EL
SICARIO

Also by Charles Bowden

Murder City

Killing the Hidden Waters

*Street Signs Chicago: Neighborhood and Other
Illusions of Big City Life* (with Lew Kreinberg)

Blue Desert

Frog Mountain Blues (photographs by
Jack W. Dykinga)

*Trust Me: Charles Keating and the Missing
Billions* (with Michael Binstein)

Mezcal

Red Line

Desierto: Memories of the Future

The Sonoran Desert (photographs by
Jack W. Dykinga)

The Secret Forest (photographs by
Jack W. Dykinga)

*Blood Orchid: An Unnatural History of
America*

Chihuahua: Pictures from the Edge
(photographs by Virgil Hancock)

Stone Canyons of the Colorado Plateau
(photographs by Jack W. Dykinga)

The Sierra Pinacate (by Julian D. Hayden;
photographs by Jack Dykinga; with essays by
Charles Bowden and Bernard L. Fontana)

Juárez: The Laboratory for Our Future
(preface by Noam Chomsky; afterword by
Eduardo Galeano)

*Down by the River: Drugs, Money, Murder,
and Family*

Blues for Cannibals

*A Shadow in the City: Confessions of an
Undercover Drug Warrior*

Inferno (photographs by Michael P. Berman)

Exodus/Éxodo (photographs by Julián Cardona)

*Some of the Dead Are Still Breathing: Living
in the Future*

Trinity (photographs by Michael P. Berman)

EL SICARIO

THE AUTOBIOGRAPHY OF A
MEXICAN ASSASSIN

EDITED BY

MOLLY MOLLOY AND
CHARLES BOWDEN

TRANSLATED AND TRANSCRIBED
BY MOLLY MOLLOY

NATION
BOOKS

New York

For my father, NDM, 1920–1998,
and my brother, NDM Jr., 1951–2010,
lovers of flight, books, and hard truths

—MM

Published by Nation Books, A Member of the Perseus Books Group
Nation Books is a co-publishing venture of
the Nation Institute and the Perseus Books Group.

Books published by Nation Books are available at special discounts for bulk purchases in the United States by corporations, institutions, and other organizations. For more information, please contact the Special Markets Department at the Perseus Books Group, 2300 Chestnut Street, Suite 200, Philadelphia, PA 19103, or call (800) 810-4145, ext. 5000, or e-mail special.markets@perseusbooks.com.

Lyrics from "Gotta Serve Somebody" by Bob Dylan
Copyright © 1979 by Special Rider Music. All rights reserved.

Lyrics from "Knockin' on Heaven's Door" by Bob Dylan
Copyright © 1973 by Ram's Horn Music; renewed 2001 by Ram's Horn Music.

Typeset in 11.75 point Adobe Garamond Pro

Library of Congress Cataloging-in-Publication Data
Sicario.
  El Sicario : the autobiography of a Mexican assassin / [edited and translated by] Molly Molloy, Charles Bowden.
    p. cm.
  Includes bibliographical references.
  ISBN 978-1-56858-658-8 (pbk.)—ISBN 978-1-56858-668-7 (e-book) 1. Sicario. 2. Assassins—Mexican-American Border Region—Biography. 3. Drug dealers—Mexican-American Border Region—Biography. 4. Drug traffic—Mexican-American Border Region. I. Molloy, Molly. II. Bowden, Charles, 1945– III. Title.
  HV6535.M42M496 2011
  364.152'4092—dc22
  [B]
                                                          2011008833
10 9 8 7 6 5 4 3 2 1

CONTENTS

Well, it may be the devil or it may be the Lord,
But you're gonna have to serve somebody.

—BOB DYLAN

CHARLES BOWDEN

He is difficult to remember. I have been dealing with him for the better part of a year when the next rendezvous happens. As usual, he is late. The meetings are always complicated and never happen on time. He keeps calling, changing times and locations, and still, every new schedule is overturned and the clock keeps ticking. I have gotten used to these complications.

But what keeps bothering me is that I cannot remember him. The face always remains a blank in my mind.

He'll be standing in front of me explaining something to me. Cars roll by on a busy avenue, and somehow he talks and yet constantly scans everything flickering around him. That time, he wanted me to understand a hit, realize that there was a long back story and he knew that story. He tells of a house in Ciudad Chihuahua, where a woman was held for five days, and how in order to convince her husband, three fingers were cut off the wife's hand on a one-a-day plan. He gives me documents so that I will understand what he is talking about. And then he gets into a truck I have never seen before and leaves.

Eventually, this passes, this failure on my part to clearly remember what he looks like. I slowly forge a face despite his ability to seemingly morph before my eyes. Part of this comes from the fact that I cannot accurately describe him in print without putting his life at risk. But mainly it comes from something else: He looks ordinary. Nothing in his appearance signals what he has been and what he has done. I think we often use words like "evil" and "monster" in order to not admit that people like the sicario are normal and just like you or me. Somehow, even given this fact, they manage to kidnap people, torture them, kill them, cut them up, and bury them when the rest of us cannot imagine doing such things.

I remember explaining this fact to a reporter from the daily newspaper in Milan, Italy, after the film that forged the core of this book had premiered in Venice. She started shouting, "No, no, no, no, no."

This account is, to my knowledge, a rare opportunity to meet such a person and to finally understand such a person. It is neither a defense of such a life nor a judgment on it, but an explanation given by a man who has done all these things and, at least for the moment, has lived to tell the tale.

This book resulted from days of interviews. Some parts have been rearranged but not much. He is a very lucid man. I remember the first interview: I asked one question, and he talked for two days without stumbling. Like most stories people make of their lives, his account is a journey from innocence to sin and then on to redemption, in his case by being born again in Christ. But it is his story—it is a Mexican life, not an American life.

The interviews began as a report that wound up in *Harper's* magazine and then continued as a film, a documentary of his life, directed by the Italian filmmaker Gianfranco Rosi. This book began with the transcripts from that filming, which went on for days on two separate occasions. He was paid for these interviews. I don't think they changed what he said or what he believes, but the reader will be the judge of that.

I believe he is going to be a part of our future. Killers like him are multiplying. The global economy has brought ruin for many, and he is a pioneer of a new type of person: the human who kills and expects to be killed and has little hope or complaint. He does not fit our beliefs or ideas. But he exists, and so do the others who are following in this path.

His story is about power, but he is never really in control. He must worry about his superiors, he must worry about other killers, about police, the army, all the agents of violence who at times are his colleagues but who never can be trusted. He must worry. His world is not as imagined in novels and films. He is always the man who comes and takes you and tortures you and kills you. But still, he is always worried, because his work stands on a floor of uncertainty. Alliances shift, colleagues vanish—sometimes because he murders them—and he seldom knows what is really going on. He catches only glimpses of the battlefield.

Since my original piece in *Harper's*, there have been some questions.

Some say that I made him up.

You be the judge.

Some ask me if he is a psychopath or sociopath or some other path.

No.

Some tell me they hope he burns in hell. Almost always this is said by those who believe neither in heaven nor in hell.

I do not share their appetite.

Some ask me if I was afraid.

Yes, of what he told me, and of what I must face as part of my world and my hopes for my world.

In 2007, 307 people were murdered in Juárez, a city that was then 348 years old. This was the bloodiest year in the history of the city.

In 2008, 1,623 people were murdered.

In 2009, 2,754 were murdered.

In 2010, 3,111 were murdered.

At the same time, El Paso, the Texas city facing Juárez, was experiencing ten to twenty murders a year. That number dwindled to five in 2010, and two of those were a murder-suicide.

And yet, the reports in the United States were about the risk of violence spilling over the border. There were few reports of the violence in Juárez.

The sicario's story is from an earlier time, one that pretty much ended in 2007. He worked in the innocent days when Mexico was peaceful and a success story to all the nations. He lived inside a system, and he explains just how this system worked. This system has changed now and become more violent, more corrupt, and more out of control. But it persists, and all discussions of Mexico must accept the facts of life that the sicario lived.

He's killed hundreds of people—he can't really remember them all—and he was paid very well for his work. He is highly trained and very intelligent. And I can't seem to remember his face.

I get bored waiting, and so I wander out of the Home Depot parking lot and kill time looking at barbecue grills. After a while, I go outside again and sit on a bench by the door. My eye floats over the busy parking lot—he likes places with lots of traffic to mask his arrival—studying vehicles as they prowl the lanes. I know this is a waste of time, since he changes cars with each trip. He prides himself on this fact, that no one can find him by noting his vehicle. Just as he never reveals where he is living at the moment and moves every two or three weeks, sometimes more often.

This is necessary because of footsteps. One time, he clears out just sixty minutes before the arrival of people who were looking for him.

But still, what strikes me is the blankness of his face in my mind. I have been wandering his world for over twenty years and have grown accustomed to fake names or no names, have learned never to ask certain questions and always to memorize faces, words, any clue that falls before me.

In his case, I keep coming up empty. I know his nickname because it accidentally fell from someone's lips. But I don't know his real name. I have prayed with him, but I can't identify his church. He knows a lot about me. He is a bear for research and mines the Internet with ease. This habit aids his work. For years he has made detailed studies of people he is to kidnap, torture, and kill.

This work habit underscores his caution. He knows the people who will come to kill him have the same skills and put in the same hours combing records in order to find him. His phone numbers have a very short life, his e-mail addresses shift constantly. I remember once spending days with him, and then, within an hour or two of leaving him, his phone number went dead forever. All this makes a certain sense because the price on his head is at least $250,000 and rising. Besides this fact, another criminal organization is searching for him in order to hire him.

Still, no system is perfect. Once, he is discovered and then flees well over a thousand miles until things calm down. He gets reports—I don't ask how—about the people looking for him. He always knows more than the newspapers report, and yet he seems severed from all contact with the workaday world.

The day is sunny, a weekend, and shoppers seem relaxed as they stream into the Home Depot with their patio dreams. In such a setting, he should stand out like a sore thumb, but I know he will not.

I stare at the ground in front of the bench and wait. Suddenly, someone is standing before me. I look up and am not sure who the person is.

Of course, it's him. This happens every time. He wears no disguise, no makeup, he does not vary costumes. He simply is not memorable.

We slap each other on the back, laugh, and then we move on. Plans are always changed at the last instant. We search for a place to talk and run through three locations before he insists on a certain motel and a certain room, 164. I have learned not to ask why.

Given the nature of this book, there are certain things that cannot be done. First, it is not my book or Molly Molloy's book but rather the sicario's book, and it must be told in his words without the protective screen of some narrator explaining him away. As it happens, he is an incisive and clear guide to his world, and there is no need to dress up his language. Second, we must realize this book is more like a song than a manual, and like a song it creates a reality and this reality creates all the answers. In this reality, everything is answered by two conditions: death and power. For example, in the opening kidnapping it becomes clear as the story evolves that essentially no one comes back from being snatched alive. And generally not even a corpse is returned to the families. Also, every problem is solved by graft. You lose an immigration card and presto, the fix is in and you get a new U.S. visa. The sicario takes us to the real Latin America, not a place of magical realism, but a place of murderous realism.

The purpose of the book is not to answer the reader's questions but to teach the reader a new reality, one in which an American reader's normal questions are absurd because the reader has entered a world of terror and total corruption. The reader is not staring at the face of the sicario, but into the true face of the Mexican state, and in this place no one asks if a cop is honest or corrupt, no one asks if a murder will be investigated, and no one asks for justice but simply seeks survival. In this world, the statements of American presidents about Mexico mean nothing because they insist on a Mexico that does not exist and that has never existed.

This is the gift of the book: a true voice from within the ranks of the people who actually run Mexico. This voice has been discussed by others from time to time but never actually allowed to speak before.

In some ways the book reminds me of the *Iliad*, a self-contained strange world that by its very existence upends all the lies and assumptions of our world. In the *Iliad* humans are toys for the gods' pleasure. In this book humans are toys that are tortured and murdered by unseen forces wearing the mask of the Mexican state. And in this world every Achilles or Hector learns this reality as he goes into the holes and is covered with lime.

What we have is the unspeakable nature of Mexican power, and for once it finally speaks and tells us both our fate and our ignorance of the world.

There is nothing to do but listen.

I have watched audiences deal with the documentary film that became the arena where the sicario discovered his desire to speak out. At first they are puzzled, then frightened, and when it ends they have no questions and too many answers. A Mexican director told me, "The problem is that he is too clear, too good, too convincing. No one wants to believe him."

That first bout of filming went on for two days.

And gradually he explained that room 164 was essential because this was the room where he once brought a package.

I remember the red door to the room opening. The bed, kitchenette, sitting area with chair and sofa—this looked familiar and safe. I'd been in hundreds of rooms just like it in my years on the road, and they had always been safe havens after long days of reporting on this or that.

But this time I was wrong.

We'd entered here to get some footage.

He had a different agenda.

We got a life that tore a hole in our idea of life.

He acted out what he had done in that room to that man.

I still have a hard time remembering his face.

But I don't think I'll forget his story.

INTRODUCTION

MOLLY MOLLOY

The night is warm and hazy from the refinery stacks on one side of the border, from street dust and smoke on the other side. A low sky glows dull orange. The stocky man sits on the bricks of the empty hearth in the mostly empty house. His thick arms cradle a baby, and another child bounces around him like a wood sprite, irrepressible after sneaking half a bag of Hershey's kisses while waiting for the man to get home. This child had called every few minutes on his cell phone during the hours we drove around the city. He gently scolds the kid now and puts the bag of chocolate away.

He took a circuitous route to the tract-house neighborhood, somewhere in the city. I am certain I could not get there again on my own. He will not be at this house for long anyway, or he would never have taken me there. He needed a ride back tonight because his borrowed car broke down. As we drove, he told me that his wife and children had crossed the border some time ago without legal papers, that it was another miracle of the Lord. The house is large, the window blinds bent and broken, a few pieces of cheap, castoff furniture in each room. Except for a table in the kitchen, a strong rough table that he crafted himself with leftover wood from a recent remodeling job.

On the old computer in the kitchen, he shows off some photographs of his recent handiwork—remodeled houses in neighborhoods like this one. He often leaves a house on an hour's notice and carries nothing with him but his family. His jobs must be arranged through others with the papers and the tools and the connections. He has the strong arms, skills, and hardworking attitude of an expert craftsman, and nothing else. I noticed on occasion during interviews that he would get a call from a former or prospective employer in his new survival world of odd construction jobs. His voice would instantly change from that of "the authority" to that of the submissive worker: "Yes, sir. Yes, chief. Of course, I'm here at your service. . . . What are your orders, sir?" The very same voice he used as he reenacted other jobs you will read about in this book.

Several days of recordings, about ten hours of sound, went into this book. Other than these introductory pages and a few footnotes, the words in the book are the sicario's words. Several other interviews were recorded in notebooks—he talked, I translated, and Charles Bowden wrote it down.

The first time I met him, the sicario was not happy at the idea of having to trust yet another person. In fact, he had already placed himself at risk by agreeing to talk to Bowden. Standing outside in a parking lot on a blustery day, Bowden introduces me as his body-guard. I translate: "*Dice que soy su guardaespalda.*" For a split second the man's eyes darken as he considers the possibility, knowing from experience that killers come in all sizes and the one that gets you is the person you overlook, but then the joke kicks in. Here we are—three men totaling at least 600 pounds between them and me at four-foot-eleven and about 100 pounds. The sicario's usually blank face breaks into a grin, and he laughs out loud, probably convinced by now that we are all crazy and certain that we have to be crazy to be there at all. Later, we learn that there were other crazy people at key moments in his journey, and now I believe he is convinced that we are part of a fraternity of holy fools that God has placed on his path. He believes that God has a purpose for his life, that part of this purpose is fulfilled by telling his story, and that Bowden and I are tools to make it happen.

We go to a motel for the interview. While the room is being rented, he takes me aside and asks me to tell Bowden that he will not be able to talk today, that he has important bills due and needs money up front. Nevertheless, without any money chang-ing hands, we go into the room and sit at the small wooden table while he talks for four hours. He looks at Bowden's notebook and tells him not to write anything down. Bowden writes for four hours. He takes a small notebook and green pen from me and diagrams parts of the story. At the end of the interview, I reach across the table to take the pages. He laughs and then tears the sheets into tiny bits and pockets them.

Months later, we meet to arrange the details for the film-ing. This is done as we drive around the city for several hours in another person's car. The sicario does not like to meet and talk in cafés or other public places. Before he has agreed to talk to Charles Bowden, he has researched him on the Internet, and he comes to the interview with a sheaf of downloaded pages about Bowden's books and a photograph taken in the writer's backyard. He has not met the filmmaker at this point, but he has searched the Web for information about Gianfranco Rosi also, and he brings some of those printouts with him when we meet to talk about the project.

He states his conditions: the film can never show his face, and his voice will have to be altered before the film can be shown. There are powerful people on both sides of the border looking for him. The price on his head is high. There are people he will speak of who are still alive. There are those who will never forget the face or the voice of the man who tortured them.

And so arrangements are made for the days and hours of the filming. Deciding on the place that will suit the subject and the filmmaker is more of a challenge. I think the sicario intended from the beginning to take us to room 164, but he wants us to make the choice. We spend an afternoon driving around the city visiting motels and apartments he has access to. Finally, he and Rosi agree on room 164. For the next two days, the sicario sits in the room where he once performed another job. But this time, for the camera, he talks for hours, his head shrouded in a black fishnet veil, and he draws pictures and diagrams with a thick brown pen in a large leather-bound sketchbook. The veil is the filmmaker's idea and is intended just to hide the man's face and also allow him to breathe, but it turns out to be a stroke of genius. With his head covered, the sicario enters a state of grace, as if talking to another person inside of himself. His words and emotions flow into story with hardly any need for questions. Later, I learn that Rosi's nine-year-old daughter saw a drawing of the sicario under the veil and told her father: he looks like an ancient killer. This drawing will become the poster for the documentary film *El Sicario, Room 164*.

On the day of this visit to the sicario's house, I have come with a digital voice recorder and a list of questions to help clear up some details, a few names, important dates, things recorded earlier that were unclear. We drive around the city for several hours, his hands controlling the recorder while I try to make notes. He remains fuzzy on the dates, explaining that when he found God he erased his *disco duro*, his hard drive. There are things he does not want to remember. But when his head is wrapped in the black veil, he inhabits that state of grace, and like a man hypnotized, he is able to relive his experiences and tell his story in a way that he cannot do face to face, in the light of day, in response to a list of questions.

He doesn't like the questions I ask, especially if they are written down and communicated in any way other than a face-to-face conversation. He knows that nothing he does is safe from notice, that people watch, that any carelessness could reveal his presence, and that he is running out of places to hide. So I drive to the meeting and later will transcribe another several hours of his answers. He shows me some printouts from the Internet that he says will illustrate some of his answers. But then he tells me that these explanations of "narco-messages" are "pure fantasy"—garbage posted online by fake sicarios. He wants to be sure I know the difference, that his voice is the authentic one. Then he answers the questions, and those words are here in this book.

When I first listen to the recordings made during the filming, they are so clear, and the voice so plain and alive, that I decide to write directly into English without first transcribing into Spanish text. It is the most careful listening I've ever done, and it is necessary so that the English text will have the sense, rhythm, and character of the Spanish speaker telling his compelling life story for the first time. As editors, we have made only minimal changes from the spoken words to the order in which the story is presented in this book. The first day is a chronological recounting of his life. On the second day, the sicario reflects on what that story means. He analyzes how his life fits into the system that he became a part of, that he managed to survive, and that he abandoned.

By the end of the second day, I start calling him "Professor." His treatise on the narco-trafficking system and its role in Mexican life and society is spoken in language so cogent and precise that I feel that I have attended a college lecture. Even better, there is nothing hypothetical in his presentation. He has lived his life as an integral component of the system he describes. It might be more accurate for me to call him "*Ingeniero,*" Engineer. With his words and diagrams, he constructs and then deconstructs for us the functioning of the Mexican government, the political economy of the drug business, and the technical details of its deadly system of control in which he was an enforcer for more than twenty years.

At one interview, I show him how to use a database containing more than thirty years of newspaper articles from the state of Chihuahua. He instantly figures out the system and begins to use it to find documentation for events that he knows about firsthand. One of the articles he finds is of a time when he procured the prostitutes and liquor for a party at a hotel. The party got out of hand, and the desk clerk was threatened by men brandishing guns. The sicario ended up under arrest, and the name he was using at that time was published in the newspaper even though he carried the badge of a federal policeman. His superiors told him later that the article had been removed from all of the newspaper archives. He laughs as he recalls the incident. On more than one occasion, his job was the procurement of women for parties, and his wife had always scolded him for this. I do not know if the name that was published was his real name.

He now searches the database regularly to try to keep track of a world he has left behind, but a world that still interests him. And he wants to explain that world to us as best he can. He considers it his duty that we get the story right. He knows that the Chihuahua press accounts reveal only a partial version of events he experienced, but he knows that these are links that can help to confirm the truth of the stories that he tells.

He brings more printed articles from the database to another interview—Chihuahua newspaper coverage of a massacre at a Juárez restaurant in August 1997 when six people were shot to death. Until the first drug rehabilitation center massacre in 2008, where nine people were killed,[1] this incident had been the largest mass killing in the city since the time of the Mexican revolution. The sicario's interest in the 1997 incident is focused on high officials at the time in the state of Chihuahua and their public pronouncements about the case. His personal knowledge of the people killed, the accused killers, and their relationships to people currently running the cartels and those in high state and federal government offices enables him to analyze and explain another nexus in the Mexican system of narco-power and government corruption. He remembers a photograph published at the time. The person in this photograph was a cartel figure who now has a high position in the government of the state of Chihuahua. He also reveals that a person mentioned in the articles as a witness to the 1997 crime was never apprehended and that he now lives on the U.S. side of the border. This man betrayed the major target in that killing. And the cartel contract on the man was $5 million, a prize he had tried to collect during his career as a sicario. A tale of hunter and hunted.

On this night, he tells us that his wife sometimes asks him what he will do if those hunting him try to kidnap his children. He replies, "Don't ask me that." He tells us that his ideas of justice are more in tune with the Old Testament "*ojo por ojo, diente por diente*," an eye for an eye and a tooth for a tooth, at least in terms of his responsibility as a Mexican man with a family to protect. He will kill to protect his family. But he has told his wife that he will not allow himself to be taken alive—he knows what happens to those who are taken. Suicide is not an option for him, but he would figure out a way to engineer his own murder by those who come for him. As he talks, it is clear that his efforts to leave the drug world and the killing world behind are still a work in progress. He absorbs media accounts past and present and fills in the missing and misreported facts that he knows from his long experience. He has left the drug world, but it has not left him.

A former partner still lives in Mexico. He receives messages that his old boss is looking for him. Perhaps the boss wants to talk to him about going back to work for the cartel. Reporting for this job interview could bring him either a lot of money or certain death. Such are his professional prospects.

At another interview, there is an old upright piano in the room where we meet. "Oh," he sighs, "I took piano lessons when I was a child. A teacher in Juárez had set up a school to teach kids who could only pay a little money. My mother enrolled me in the school, and it had a room full of old pianos like this one. I remember trying to learn my notes . . . do, re, mi. . . . I would hit the wrong key, and the teacher would rap me on the knuckles with a ruler. . . . He did it several times, and I finally got mad and I hit him back. Oh, he kicked me out of the school. My mother was so embarrassed. I was ten years old."

I imagine the life this man might have lived had he been born in a country where opportunities exist for a person from a working-class background with sharp intelligence, technical knowledge, analytical abilities, and a restless mind always seeking new information. He could have been an accountant, an engineer, or an architect (as his mother imagined). Or he might have chosen a career in academia or high-level law enforcement. Certainly the FBI, DEA, or CIA could have made good use of someone with his abilities. In a society possessing even the rudiments of a merit-based system, he would have been a successful man.

As this book shows, the sicario is not a fictional character, but a talented and intelligent man whose life choices were forged by the social and economic realities of his time and place. This does not excuse his decision to become a part of a murderous criminal enterprise, but in his own words, he explains his choices. And he lives every day with the consequences of those choices.

● ● ●

The sicario's account takes us inside the world of narco-trafficking and police enforcement. But there are elements of the story that require some background understanding for readers not familiar with Mexico or the intricacies of the drug trade. In the following paragraphs, I explain some important points.

THE PLAZA

Crime and government meet in the Mexican concept of the "plaza." In Mexico, the word takes on a specific sense apart from—but extending—its normal meaning of a town or city center or square. Historically, the Mexican state has allowed criminal organizations to exist while at the same time maintaining control over them by designating a liaison to supervise their activities and take a cut of their income for the state. Whoever controlled the plaza kept crime orderly and profitable for the state. There have always been variations of this concept in the United States as well. Cops take bribes to overlook backroom gambling, houses of prostitution, and bars that run past closing time. In Mexico, the relationship is much closer, and it has become more significant in recent decades. It is common knowledge that the police are corrupt and often commit crimes. With the rise of the modern drug business in the 1980s, the money earned by drug merchants skyrocketed, and the interest of the state grew in proportion to this new source of wealth. The U.S. Drug Enforcement Administration (DEA) estimates that for at least twenty years illicit drugs have earned Mexico from $30 billion to $50 billion a year. Today income from the drug trade is second only to oil in earning Mexico foreign currency—or perhaps drug income exceeds oil income, since no one really knows how much money is made in the drug business. Globally, the illegal drug industry dwarfs the auto industry.

This kind of money fosters murder. The sicario was often assigned to kill people who operated in Juárez but failed to pay for their use of the plaza. The huge profits from the booming drug industry also changed the balance of power between the government and the criminal enterprises. Until the 1980s, criminals normally approached the police and made a financial arrangement so that they could carry on their commerce. But with the billions tumbling in from cocaine, marijuana, and heroin, the criminals began to dictate the terms—the infamous *"plata o plomo,"* silver or lead. The police could either take the money offered to do the bidding of the crime syndicate, or be killed.

The sicario's job duties included delivering quantities of money from the Juárez cartel to officials in several Chihuahua state administrations during the 1990s. These payments were made to arrange the control of the plaza. He then watched as these officials rose to higher and higher positions of power in the Mexican government. When he talks about this from the place where he now hides from fellow sicarios seeking to collect the contract on his own life, his anger is palpable. He knows the corrupting power of the money that he helped to earn and distribute. And he knows that the power of many Mexican officials is paid for with the blood of hundreds of Mexicans like himself. He knows this because he has been both executioner and target.

It is difficult to exaggerate the amount of money involved in these transactions. By the mid-1990s, the banks in El Paso, Texas, across the river from Juárez, were booking deposits that exceeded the cash flow of the legitimate economy by $700 million a year. In news accounts from 1996, "U.S. authorities estimate[d] that $3.5 billion in drug profits are laundered locally through El Paso."[2] In 2007 more than $205 million was discovered stored in a single house in Mexico City belonging to Zhenli Ye Gon, a Chinese businessman involved in the importation of chemicals used in the manufacture of methamphetamine. Ye Gon later claimed that much of the money belonged to the ruling political party, the PAN, and that he was being forced to safeguard the money to be used by politicians as a slush fund.[3]

By the turn of the twenty-first century, the narco-trafficking organizations had begun to take over more and more control of legitimate society, and this change is now the face of Mexico. The sicario has lived through this evolution. In the years before he left the organization he worked for, he and his colleagues were handling shipments of drugs worth $30 million to $40 million. Such sums of money create temptation to steal, and part of the sicario's work was to kill people who attempted to cheat the boss.[4]

THE CARTELS

In the legitimate world, the word "cartel" refers to a group of businesses seeking to control a market. The antitrust laws in the United States were originally created to break cartels. The Mexican drug organizations have never been able to completely control the market and have always had to contend with smaller operators who try to compete. When discovered, these small-time capitalists are murdered. Movers and shakers in American business corporations are accustomed to working hard, making lots of money, and, at the end of their useful economic lives, they are fired or they retire with a golden parachute. Cartel executives at the same point in their careers are often executed.

A second reality is that drug cartels in Mexico are somewhat fluid. From the late 1980s to the present, several groups of various origins and shifting territories have dominated the drug business in Mexico: Sinaloa, Juárez, Gulf, Tijuana, Beltran-Leyva, Los Zetas, La Familia Michoacana. Sometimes disparate groups or subgroups of one or another of the major cartels band together on certain deals and then drift apart, or a fragment of one group will strike out on its own. There is constant friction between groups, and in the business of drugs friction produces murder.

The Juárez cartel first bloomed in the mid-1980s when cocaine shipments from South America began to stream through Mexico. The cartel had two key assets: arrangements with cocaine producers in Colombia, Peru, and Bolivia and control of the crossing into El Paso. By the late 1990s, the U.S. drug czar Barry McCaffrey estimated, fifteen tons of cocaine were being warehoused in Juárez at any given moment. As the Juárez cartel gained strength and territory during the 1990s, DEA officials estimated that the Juárez plaza generated cash surpluses in El Paso of $50 million to $70 million each month—money that circulated through the real estate and luxury goods markets on the U.S. side of the border.[5]

The key architect of this industry in Juárez was Amado Carrillo Fuentes, who controlled the plaza from May 1993 until his death in July 1997. Carrillo had arranged to have his predecessor, Rafael Aguilar Guajardo, murdered so that he could take over the job. At the height of his power, Amado Carrillo was practically untouchable. He traveled all over Mexico with a bodyguard detail composed of several dozen federal police officers. Carrillo was the first cartel boss who tried to create a structure that would foster cooperation among the various narco-trafficking organizations and thus allow the business to grow and flourish with fewer costly and bloody cartel wars. Amado Carrillo was also able to forge alliances between the drug-trafficking organizations and the highest levels of the Mexican government. When Amado Carrillo died in 1997, Peter Lupsha, a longtime scholar of organized crime and money laundering in Latin America, said: "In Colombia, the drug capos are threatening the state from the outside. In Mexico, they're part of the state."[6]

Carrillo's brother Vicente took over after Amado's death in a Mexican hospital in 1997, where he underwent plastic surgery to change his appearance. Don Vicente Carrillo continues to run the organization today. By all accounts, he keeps a much lower profile than his brother did, which perhaps has contributed to his unprecedented longevity at the helm of the Juárez cartel. The sicario met Vicente Carrillo when he was about fifteen years old, and his entire career was interwoven with this major narco-trafficking organization. As a young man, the sicario worked as part of a security detail for the men at the highest levels in the cartel, and he describes how he and his coworkers were required to maintain complete devotion to these bosses. From his account, one learns of the power of the cartel, and also of the constant tension and instability created by rival groups seeking to take over the plaza or by those within the cartel seeking to cheat the organization. The sicario never felt secure, always slept with loaded guns by his bed, and expected to be killed at any time. He saw fellow cartel workers rise and fall, and he was often ordered to execute people he had worked with.

As he tells his story, we realize that the sicario was never sure exactly who he was working for and seldom received orders from people much higher in the organization than himself. He describes in some detail the cartel's cell structure, a form of organization that kept information strictly compartmentalized and controlled. But during the last years of his tenure with the Juárez cartel—2006 to 2007—this level of control began to break down, and the sicario was no longer sure who gave the orders.

It was also during this period that a larger struggle began to take place, one usually described as the attempt by *"la gente nueva,"* the new people, associated with the Sinaloa cartel, led by Joaquin "El Chapo" Guzman, to take control of the Juárez plaza. In December 2006, President Calderón announced that the Mexican military would be called on to fight against the drug cartels, even though there is ample evidence that the army had been in league with traffickers going back several decades.[7] A new period of hyperviolence would begin in Mexico, and by 2008 Ciudad Juárez had become the bloody epicenter of this conflict.

PRESIDENT CALDERÓN'S WAR

On December 1, 2006, Felipe Calderón assumed the presidency of Mexico after barely winning the elections and enduring a period of challenges by his opposition in the congress. Stolen elections in Mexico are a national tradition, and many citizens see Calderón as an illegitimate ruler. Shortly after taking office, Calderón posed in military uniform—something taboo in Mexico since the revolution. His move to deploy 45,000 soldiers to fight the drug cartels was interpreted by many as a tactic to give a boost to his contested and very weak presidency—a bold move to prove that he possessed *"la mano dura,"* the hard hand.

The presence of the military on the streets greatly increased the level of violence in many areas of Mexico. Many Mexicans began to notice that the Sinaloa cartel, headed by Joaquin "El

Chapo" Guzman, seemed relatively untouched by the military campaign. People began to suspect that the army was fighting, not against the cartels, but on the side of one, with the goal of consolidating control over a larger share of the huge profits generated by the drug business and especially by the Juárez plaza. Edgardo Buscaglia, a lawyer and organized crime expert in Mexico City, analyzed public security statistics and determined that "only 941 of the 53,174 people arrested for organized crime in the past six years were associated with Sinaloa."[8] National Public Radio also examined official arrest data from the Mexican federal attorney general's office dating from the beginning of Calderón's term through May 2010. This investigation showed that only 12 percent of 2,600 federal defendants accused of being cartel operatives were associated with the Sinaloa organization.[9] A former Juárez police commander seeking asylum in the United States said, speaking anonymously to a Canadian journalist, that several smuggling gangs in the city split from the Juárez cartel in 2007 and joined forces with the Sinaloa organization, which was in the process of trying to take over this lucrative plaza. These shifting alliances spawned a great deal of the killing that exploded in the city in early 2008.[10] There is off-the-record speculation from people in the DEA that nothing bad will happen to El Chapo while President Calderón is in office. And as is often the case in Mexico, rumor becomes fact, suspicion substitutes for thought, and both rumor and suspicion may sometimes be closer to the truth than public facts.

Verifiable facts about the relationship between Calderón's government, the military, and the cartels are difficult to come by, but there is no doubt that Ciudad Juárez is ground zero in the slaughter being generated across Mexico. After four years of sporadic and vague official releases on the carnage in its drug wars, in January 2011 the Mexican government issued a new report (accompanied by data sets) stating that 34,612 homicides linked to narco-trafficking have occurred since Calderón took office in December 2006 and that the numbers have increased each year at ever higher rates.[11] As posted by Johanna Tuckman in a report in *The Guardian*, Juárez has been the most violent city since 2008 despite the military presence there. *The Guardian* also makes the important caveat that "the figures released do not specify how many of those killed are presumed to be related to the cartels, how many belonged to the security forces, or how many were innocent civilians dragged into the horror."[12]

Larger estimates ranging up to nearly 50,000 dead were reported in early 2011 in different Mexican media.[13] This is out of a total population of 112,468,855.[14] Between one-fifth and one-quarter of all of Mexico's dead have been killed in Juárez, a city of between 1.2 and 1.3 million people.

At the time when the sicario engineered his escape from the system in 2007, Juárez was in the middle of a record-breaking year of murder that ended with a reported toll of 307 homicides. Murders increased fivefold in 2008, for a total of 1,623 victims. Also in 2008, 45 bodies came out of the ground during excavations at several death houses, but these deaths have never been officially assigned to the murder numbers for any year, since there is no official information about when these murders occurred. In 2009 there were 2,754 homicides in the city, and 2010 ended with 3,111 murder victims, as reported in *El Diario de Juárez*— an average of 8.5 murders per day. October 2010 set a record of 359 homicides in one month. The murder rate in Juárez is now estimated to be the highest of any city in the world, more than

250 per 100,000 people, a rate that increased 800 percent between 2007 and 2010. As of February 21, 2011, another 384
people had died, bringing the total number of Juárez victims in
the four years of Calderon's war to more than 8,000.[15]

It makes no sense to attribute all of this killing to a cartel
war. If this is a war, then who are the combatants? Since early
2008, more than 8,000 soldiers and federal police have patrolled
the Juárez streets. The newspapers seldom report on the number
of soldiers killed, and the Mexican military does not normally
release information on casualties. During all of 2008 and 2009,
Juárez newspapers only reported three soldiers killed in the city.
A government report in August 2010 revealed that a total of 191
military personnel and 2,076 federal, state, and municipal police
in all of Mexico had been killed since Calderón launched his
war,[16] and the total number of dead reported in August was
28,000. In the January 2011 report, the government numbers
do not specify which ones of the dead were members of the military or other security forces.

The most salient information to be gleaned from these government releases is that they probably report a minimum number
of the deaths that have occurred. We also know that when President Calderón or other government spokesmen say that 90 percent of the dead are criminals, it is also the case that fewer than
5 percent of the crimes have been investigated.[17] And by reading
the daily accounts of murders in the Juárez newspapers, one sees
that the overwhelming majority of the victims are ordinary
people and that most of them are poor: children, teenagers, old
people, small-business proprietors who refused to pay extortion
demands, mechanics, bus drivers, a woman selling burritos from
a cart on the street, a clown juggling at an intersection, boys selling newspapers, gum, and perhaps nickel bags of cocaine or

heroin on a street corner, an increasing number of young women who are taking jobs in the drug business, and dozens of people who have been slaughtered inside drug rehabilitation clinics. Social workers have estimated that there are between 150,000 and 200,000 addicts just in the city of Juárez. At one point in his story, the sicario speaks to the increasing numbers of poor people using and dealing drugs in Juárez and the devastating impact of this growing small-time domestic retail market.

People call many of the victims *"malandros,"* bad guys, riffraff, human garbage. Sometimes they use the phrase *"limpieza social,"* social cleansing, to describe these killings. The truth is that fewer than 5 percent of homicides in Mexico will ever be investigated or solved.[18] But what is increasingly clear is that if this is a war, it is being waged, at least in part, by powerful forces of the Mexican government against poor and marginalized sectors of the Mexican people.

In October 2010, a potential bombshell hit the Mexican press when a national newspaper, *El Universal*, published an article entitled "Social Cleansing, Not Drug War." According to the article, "legislators say the state permits the existence of death squads. . . . Due to massive numbers of executions, the Senate of the Republic asks for reports on the existence of death squads."[19] The article details the efforts of a few Mexican senators from an opposition party to force the internal intelligence branch of the government (CISEN) to release a report that contained evidence of the existence of paramilitary death squads implicated in many of the killings. Spokesmen for civic organizations that monitor human rights in the states of Chihuahua, Sinaloa, Sonora, Tamaulipas, Zacatecas, Nuevo Leon, and Baja California spoke of deaths and disappearances that have never been reported: "The silence is terrible. No account is given of what actually happens and if it were possible to reveal these 'black operations' we would see that there are not 28,000 dead as the government says, but rather, more than 40,000." The article alleges that deserters from the army and police—many who had been dismissed for corruption—make up these squads of killers and "operate dressed in official uniforms, driving patrol cars, and with weapons, badges and keys just like the forces of the state." A human rights lawyer in Baja California said that the extermination squads have been named "black commandos." "We cannot just talk about groups of thugs, gunmen, sicarios and drug trafficking activities; these accusations imply the full participation of the state."

The article was ignored by the international media, and there was practically no follow-up in the Mexican press. Yet its revelations read like a chapter from the sicario's story.

VICTOR MANUEL OROPEZA

On July 3, 1991, Juárez dentist and newspaper columnist Victor Manuel Oropeza was stabbed to death in his office. The murder has never been solved, despite forensic evidence and eyewitnesses who reported seeing four men enter and leave Oropeza's office on the evening of the killing. Dr. Oropeza was a prominent member of Juárez society, and his murder generated considerable media coverage—more than four hundred articles in Chihuahua newspapers alone in the eighteen years since the killing, as well as mention in the international press. Several suspects were arrested and held for some months, but they were freed owing to the fact that they were tortured into confessing and later questioning revealed that they had no knowledge of the actual circumstances of the crime. Some of the state police officials who took charge of the investigation were individuals whom Dr.

Oropeza had written about in the months and weeks preceding his murder, accusing them of involvement in drug trafficking in Juárez. According to some press accounts, the officers responsible for the investigation were suspects in the killing.[20]

Over the years, in addition to several botched investigations by the Chihuahua state prosecutor and the Mexican attorney general, Oropeza's murder has been the subject of inquiries by the Mexican National Human Rights Commission, the Inter American Press Association, and the Organization of American States.

The sicario's interest in the case is detailed in his story. The murder occurred early in his career in the Chihuahua state police, and he was part of a team that provided protection for the hit men. Because of his job at the time, he knows that the allegations made by Oropeza in his columns were true. He also identifies the murder as one of the first successful attempts by drug cartel operatives to silence anyone who drew attention to the expanding and increasingly systemic links between the criminal organizations, the police, and the Mexican state. It is worth noting that on January 2, 1992, *El Norte de Ciudad Juárez* published a roundup of "one of the most violent years in the history of Juárez": in 1991, the year that included the killing of Oropeza, there were a total of 134 murders in the city.[21]

The person the sicario identifies as the mastermind of the murder, El Cora de Sinaloa, does not appear in any press account that I could find, but this is not surprising.[22] Mexican newspapers seldom report any news that is not sanctioned by both narco-trafficking groups and the government. The Committee to Protect Journalists consistently ranks Mexico as one of the most dangerous countries for journalists in the Western Hemisphere. According to Reporters Without Borders, at least sixty-seven Mexican journalists have been killed since 2000, while another eleven have gone missing. Those who threaten, kidnap, and kill journalists are almost never punished for their crimes.[23]

GENERAL REBOLLO

Mexican Army general Jesús Gutiérrez Rebollo was appointed by President Ernesto Zedillo in December 1996 to be Mexico's top anti-narcotics officer or "drug czar." At the time of his appointment, he was in charge of the military region that included Guadalajara, and he had a clean reputation according to U.S. officials from DEA and other agencies. In retrospect, however, it was evident that he had focused most of his enforcement efforts on drug cartel activities in Tijuana and consistently ignored Juárez. Suspicions were aroused when General Rebollo rented an apartment in Mexico City that appeared to be far too luxurious for his military salary. Investigations found that the apartment actually belonged to Amado Carrillo.[24]

At the time, Rebollo had access to all of Mexico's classified drug enforcement information, police records, and informants, and it is assumed that he passed this information on to Amado Carrillo. His arrest in February 1997 on charges of bribery, perverting the course of justice, facilitating the transportation of cocaine, and directly aiding Amado Carrillo proved extremely embarrassing to the United States, since just a few weeks before, he had been welcomed to Washington by the U.S. drug czar, Barry McCaffrey, who praised his honesty, integrity, and skills in pursuing drug traffickers. During that visit, the DEA shared sensitive intelligence with General Rebollo, probably endangering the lives of informants in Mexico. As frequently happens with high profile arrests in Mexico, the conviction may not match the publicized charges. In the case of General Rebollo, the DEA reported in 1998 that he was convicted and sentenced to thirteen years and nine months in jail for unauthorized use of firearms.[25] Rebollo was the model for the character of General Salazar in the 2001 Oscar-winning movie *Traffic*.[26]

The sicario uses the case of General Rebollo to illustrate the long-standing relationships between the Mexican drug-trafficking organizations and the military, although he believes that this case was unusual at the time. He noted a change at high-level gatherings during his tenure with the cartel: military officers began to show up regularly at fiestas in rural areas in Chihuahua where he had helped to provide women and other entertainments. He estimates that this change took place sometime in 2003.

JOSE LUIS SANTIAGO VASCONCELOS AND JUAN CAMILO MOURIÑO

Several times in his story, the sicario mentions the significance of the work that Señor Jose Luis Santiago Vasconcelos did from his position as an assistant prosecutor in the federal attorney general's office in Mexico. According to the sicario, Vasconcelos played a major role in bringing clandestine burials to light, as well as in other actions that served to damage narco-trafficking organizations, before his death in a plane crash in Mexico City on November 4, 2008. An obituary in *The Guardian* noted that Vasconcelos "came face to face with some of the most infamous of Mexico's trafficking barons." Vasconcelos pursued the extraditions of several major cartel figures to the United States, and he made many enemies among Mexican politicians through his investigations of money laundering. His life was threatened numerous times, but he "retained a reputation for being above corruption."[27] The powerful secretary of *Gobernación* (Interior), Juan Camilo

Mouriño, was also killed in the plane crash. Before his death, Vasconcelos had been moved to a less prominent job that took him out of the front lines of the drug war. Though the Calderón government denied that the deaths of these two men had any connection to their roles as prominent fighters of organized crime, most Mexicans, including the sicario, believe that both Mouriño and Vasconcelos were targeted for challenging the power of the drug traffickers.

Although they never met, the sicario indicates that he had considered seeking help from Vasconcelos during the period when he was attempting to escape from his life as a cartel enforcer. The sicario's career was marked at its beginning and its end by his encounters with two men he perceived as making real and honest efforts to expose the crimes of the Mexican state: the crusading journalist Oropeza and the vigilant government crimefighter Vasconcelos. He bookends his own story with the object lessons represented by these two individuals.

• • •

Just after midnight on January 31, 2010, a commando of armed and hooded men drove several trucks into the Villas del Salvárcar neighborhood in Juárez, blocked off the street, and machine-gunned several dozen people, most of them teenagers attending a dance party at a small house. Sixteen people died. Government officials, including President Calderón, immediately accused the victims of being gangsters killed by rival gangsters—allegations that were challenged by the mothers of the victims, who as it turned out were mostly athletes and honor students. A few days later, several men who were identified as working for La Linea— enforcers for the Juárez cartel—were arrested and confessed to participating in the massacre, though it seems that they attacked this party by mistake. As usual when the government claims it is solving a crime, those who confessed in front of the media looked to have been severely beaten shortly before they faced the cameras. Asked to comment on this event, the sicario says:

> Everything is all stirred up and like the saying, "from the turbulent river, the fishermen profit." It doesn't matter that they do not know where to find Number 10 [the man said to have ordered the operation], and the people, what do they have except this? Who knows how many more lies this arrested person is going to tell? The pressure is very strong right now because so many innocent people died. There is no longer any respect for anyone. No one is coordinating anything. It just gets worse and worse. But in the end, the police chiefs continue to collect money from whoever comes, not taking into account the damage that they are causing. These people who were arrested are not well-known people. They seem to lack any expertise, and they do not use professional techniques. They are just imitators. I hope that they get them all quickly before they cause more damage.

The sicario is adamant that despite the explosion of violence and killing that has taken place since his flight across the border several years ago, the flow of drugs continues as before. He says that he knows the deputy of the Carrillo Fuentes organization, who is now in charge of getting drug shipments over the border into the United States. Searching aerial photos on Google Earth, he can identify the drug *bodegas* (warehouses) that are used on both sides of the line and see that the eighteen-wheeler traffic to and from these facilities continues unimpeded. And the thousands of people killed on the streets in the past three years just don't matter to the drug-trafficking organizations because these are not the people who generate the money. He thinks that the atmosphere of unrestrained violence acts as a smokescreen for the real business and that the money flow is now better than ever.

In October 2010, a series of videos appeared online featuring the brother of a former Chihuahua attorney general stating that both he and his sister worked in the upper echelons of the Juárez cartel and that his sister ordered and/or facilitated many of the high-profile killings of police, journalists, politicians, and political activists in Chihuahua in recent years. In the video, the man sits handcuffed, surrounded by men wearing black masks and camouflage and pointing automatic rifles at his head and body. His sister is indignant and claims that the kidnapping and video are the work of state police officers whom she fired for corruption, but she also says that the video appears to have been filmed in a room in the state police headquarters in Juárez; she knows this because she recognizes the painted walls as part of a renovation project she presided over. A few days later, her brother's body turns up half buried on a ranch in a rural area of the state, and the family refuses to claim him until DNA tests prove his identity.[28]

A friend in Juárez who works in a media outlet writes that "there are days when I simply can't handle the anxiety that something new and very very bad will happen and then, I confess to you, I pray and ask God to take care of all of my family and all those I love. And then . . . that video. . . . Could there be a better demonstration of the total decomposition of the Mexican political system?"

A month later, twenty more bodies, including three women and at least one man buried with U.S. identity documents, came out of the ground near the tiny border town of Palomas, Chihuahua. The bodies were taken to the morgue in Juárez, and the government issued an invitation to those with missing relatives to help identify the bodies. These dead could not be counted as the victims of a certain month or year, because no information was released about when they might have been buried. One family from New Mexico went to the morgue in Juárez to identify their missing loved one. When they left the facility, they said that the Mexican Army was involved in his disappearance because a GPS signal located his cell phone at the military headquarters near Palomas.[29]

· · ·

It is a rare person who can tell a clear and true life story. It is even rarer to encounter a person who has lived within the drug world who has such facility with words and the clarity of mind to tell his story. Most participants in this system do not talk about it. No one inside of the system could talk about it and live. The few who leave have a much better chance of survival if they maintain silence.

Charles Bowden learned of the sicario through a confidential source who had provided him with a hiding place after his escape from the cartel. Another confidential source who had worked in the police and for the cartel knew the sicario's past, and this person also vouched for his experience. The sicario is not telling his story to accrue accolades or glory—he insists that neither his face nor his voice nor his name can be made known. His words contain no exaggeration or bragging. He never admits to knowing more than he has actually experienced. When he speaks of things he has only heard of, or when he speculates, he takes care to qualify these statements as such. Having never been charged with a crime, he has no reason to bargain with any law enforcement agency. Thus, when we are asked why the sicario has chosen to tell this story, we believe his own explanation: that he speaks from the sense of duty that comes from his conversion to Christianity. He believes that God gave him new life and that he must use it to tell others in the drug world that salvation is possible. He wants to atone for some of his deeds by explaining how the Mexican system really works.

In a recent conversation, the sicario said to us:

> I thought long and hard before I talked to Chuck [Bowden], and now he has become my accomplice. I asked God, "Why should I trust him?" I needed to make someone else part of this so that I could be at peace. I asked God to give me a sign, and He did, and I decided that I would trust Chuck with the story of the things that I had done. In the beginning I did not trust him, but I knew where he lived, so that if anything happened to my family, I could find him. It was hard later on to realize I would have to trust another person, the translator, but in order to tell the story the right way, I needed Molly also. I talked to an adviser in my church, but other Christians already know that God can save a sicario. I want the people of the world and especially other sinners to know.

During this conversation, the sicario also said that being able to talk about his life with us has given him a sense of relief. "These are not things that I can talk about with my wife." He has thrown a little of the dirt our way. He has involved us, he has wrapped us up in these stories. Through talking to us, he has found a way to share a part of the burden, to not be so alone with his past.[30] Regardless of his motivation, it is the sicario's ability with words that opens the window into an unknown world.

You may ask, "Why should I believe that God's salvation is available to a man who has committed such crimes?" I answer that this is *his* belief, which he is able to explain clearly and completely. He believes that he has been saved by God's grace and that he is alive because God's purpose for him is to lead others away from such a life. He has much to atone for, and he is a mere baby in terms of learning to live a Christian life. He begins from nothing and possesses nothing at the end. He believes that the only source of forgiveness is the grace and power of God. And although the sicario knows that God has the power to forgive, he is never absolutely certain that he can be forgiven because of the terrible things that he has done.

• • •

On one occasion, the sicario took Gianfranco Rosi and me to a youth service at a giant church near the border. A converted warehouse on the outskirts of the city, the place was originally built to accommodate eighteen-wheelers loading and unloading the goods of free trade. Hundreds of evaporative coolers churn on the metal roof and blast the space with slightly chilled air. The huge windowless room is now outfitted with several thousand folding chairs, and on this summer afternoon the parking lot fills with cars from Texas, New Mexico, Arizona, California, Nevada, Michigan, Tennessee, South Carolina, Chihuahua, Sonora, and other Mexican states.

The church is hosting a youth festival, and the sicario is running the lights and sound for a Christian rock concert. Outside the sun bakes blinding white on acres of concrete and corrugated metal, but inside near total darkness precedes the opening chords of the rock band and then an explosion of color and sound. He raises his arms in praise, singing along to the words projected onto a giant screen over the stage. He wanted Gianfranco to film him at his job here and to see this work that he contributes to the church that he credits for his salvation.

I believe in his conversion and in his commitment to Christianity for another important reason: it is a liability for him to be a Christian. His beliefs now forbid him to kill, yet the people looking for him will kill him on sight, and they will not hesitate to kidnap his family as a way to get to him. His beliefs compel him to tell his story in an effort to save others in the life, and thus he takes much greater risks than if he maintained silence. His beliefs compel him to try to atone for his sins, and he does this through work in his church. As I watched him that afternoon at the concert, I realized that he spends a lot of time here and that he has many friends. And yet every person he knows and every hour he spends in large gatherings and public places puts him at risk. Every word that he spoke to us in those rooms and all of the words recorded in these pages place him in greater danger.

During the two years we have been working on this project, the sicario has had to curtail some of his public activities, including going to church. As the violence escalates in Juárez, increasing numbers of people have come to live on the U.S. side of the border, including some with ties to criminal organizations. It is only a matter of time before someone recognizes him, and every appearance he makes in public puts him and his family at greater risk. Because of his former jobs, he knows that he is only one mistake away from being the captive rather than the captor. He must hide from the criminals in the world he once inhabited—people just like himself—and his life on this side must remain invisible to any official entity of government, else he will be deported to a certain death.

• • •

On this evening we drive to the sicario's temporary home. My guide and our host indulge in a bit of gallows humor as we get out of the car, a little something to remind me of the other houses in the story of his life that we are writing: "Ay! Molly, now we are going to kidnap you." And I moan and they laugh. This truly is a fraternity of holy fools. The sicario carries in his head a rich geography of safe houses and death houses in Mexico where he has kidnapped, tortured, killed, and buried people. He has also held people on the U.S. side of the border and then delivered them to their deaths in Juárez.

We go inside and meet the sicario's family. Someone brings me a glass of tap water, and I get to hold the baby for a few minutes. The baby was another character in the drama of the motel room where the sicario told the story: the arrangements were carefully planned to allow him to get to his wife's side in a matter of minutes should he get a call.

He once called distraught because the baby could be born at any time and the hospital required a special newborn infant seat for his car or he would not be allowed to drive the baby home and at the moment he did not have the money to buy it. I procured the infant seat from a big-box store and delivered it to him the next day. Later, I saw the baby's picture, along with a photograph of a bleak highway, dark clouds and a faint rainbow arching over it. And he had written these words:

Children are an inheritance from The Lord.
The fruits of the womb are our reward.

Whenever our meetings end, whether in a motel room or driving around the city, there is a prayer. This night, it is past ten, and we gather in a circle in the bare room with the computer, a broken table, and an empty refrigerator. The mother holds the baby. I put one arm around her on my right, the other around the man on my left, and the man to his left spreads his large arms over the little group and leads the prayer. The baby squirms and cries a little, and I rub its fuzzy head.

My guide on this night is a mentor to the sicario, one of the men who counseled him at the beginning of his Christian journey. He is a man whom I trust with my life. He drives me back to my car, very slowly across the entire length of the city. Tonight his usually jovial nature seems darker and sadder than I have known before. We talk about the two cities and the two countries, these lives and their struggles on the line. When I get to my car to continue my drive home, I think of calling and asking him to pray for us all. But I know he will have done that already.

A NOTE ON THE ORGANIZATION OF THIS BOOK

In the pages that follow, except for footnotes and some intermittent text in italics, the words were all spoken or written by the sicario. The story begins with a reenactment of the incident that brought the sicario to room 164 at some point in his past. The next long section is the story of his life as he told it for the camera, during one sitting of about four hours. He divided his life into the segments that we have used as chapter titles: "Child," "Teenager," "Man," and "Child of God." These are his labels.

On the second day of filming, we began by asking him to explain a few points in more detail. Other than a few scribbled notes that he carried, he spoke without pause, breaking only when Gianfranco Rosi, the documentary director, needed to change cartridges or batteries or angles or some other technical aspect of the filming. For four hours or so, he talked as if he were giving a university lecture on how the Mexican system works.

He also reflected on his own behavior and on how drugs and violence became his way of life. He analyzed how he manipulated these aspects of his way of life to engineer his escape from the system. Several other sessions were recorded on a digital voice recorder while we drove around the city with the sicario, listening as he answered questions and reflected on certain aspects of his life. These sections are arranged in the second part of the book as alternating segments of "The System" and "The Life."

NOTES

1. Molly Molloy, "Massacre at CIAD #8 in Juárez," Narco News Bulletin, August 18, 2008, http://www.narconews.com/Issue54/article3181.html. In 2009 there were more massacres at rehab centers that killed up to twenty people in single attacks. Also, in 2010, there were attacks on parties in private homes in Juárez that resulted in up to sixteen people being killed in multiple separate incidents.

2. Charles Bowden, *Down by the River: Drugs, Money, Murder, and Family* (New York: Simon & Schuster, 2002), p. 183. According to Bowden, this estimate of drug money in El Paso banks came from conversations with local DEA officials in the mid-1990s. See also "U.S. Investigates Money Laundering in El Paso," *Frontera Norte Sur*, October 1996, http://www.nmsu.edu/~frontera/old_1996/oct96/ 1096laun.html. *Frontera Norte Sur* cites articles from the *El Paso Times* and *Diario de Juárez.*

3. Karin Brulliard, "In Tale of Millionaire Drug Suspect, Mexicans Judge Government Guilty," *Washington Post*, July 29, 2007.

4. For a snapshot of the Mexican drug trade and government corruption in the mid- to late 1990s, see U.S. House of Representatives Government Reform and Oversight Committee, National Security, International Affairs, and Criminal Justice Subcommittee, statement by Thomas A. Constantine, Administrator, Drug Enforcement Administration, U.S. Department of Justice, in DEA congressional testimony before the hearing regarding cooperation with Mexico, February 25, 1997, http://www.justice.gov/dea/pubs/cngrtest/ct970225.htm#Effect%20of%20 Mexican%20Organized%20Crime%20on%20United%20States. See also Terrence E. Poppa, *Druglord: The Life and Death of a Mexican Kingpin*, 3rd ed. (El Paso, Texas: Cinco Puntos, 2010) for a singular account of Pablo Acosta's control of the plaza in the city of Ojinaga, Chihuahua, in the 1980s—the period preceding the rise of Amado Carrillo and the Juárez cartel.

5. Robert Draper, "Carrillo's Crossing," *Texas Monthly* 23, no. 12, December 1995.

6. Phil Gunson, "End of the Line: This Is the Face of Amado Carrillo Fuentes— and It May Have Cost Him His Life," *The Guardian* (London), July 17, 1997, p. T2.

7. Carlos Fazio, "Mexico: The Narco General Case," *Transnational Institute*, December 1997, http://www.tni.org/article/mexico-narco-general-case. Another Wikileaks cable surfaced in the Mexican and international press in February 2011 with the title: "Mexican Army Major Arrested for Assisting Drug Trafficking Organizations." The cable was written by U.S. Ambassador Tony Garza and is dated January 20, 2009. It mentions the arrest in December 2008 of Mexican Army Major Arturo Gonzalez Rodriguez, a member of President Calderon's protective service, for his links to drug traffickers. The cable also indicates that narco-trafficking organizations obtained access to President Calderon's medical records. See http://www.jornada.unam.mx/ultimas/2011/02/21/en-manos-de-carteles-del-narco-datos-confidenciales-de-felipe-calderon and http://www.laht.com/article.asp?ArticleId=387742&CategoryId=14091. The full text of the cable is available here: http://wikileaks.ch/cable/2009/01/09MEXICO133.html.

8. "Outsmarted by Sinaloa," *The Economist* 394, no. 8664, January 9, 2010, 40–41.

9. John Burnett, Marisa Peñalosa, and Robert Benincasa, "Mexico Seems to Favor Sinaloa Cartel in Drug War," National Public Radio, May 19, 2010, http://www.npr.org/templates/story/story.php?storyId=126906809. This NPR report quotes Mexican officials, academics, journalists, and U.S. law enforcement personnel—on and off the record—all of whom cite examples of the Sinaloa cartel's relationships with the military and high government officials and its relatively advantageous position during the years of the Calderón administration.

10. Bruce Livesey, "Drug War or Drug Deal? Mexico's Biggest Cartel Banks on Powerful Friends," *Montreal Gazette*, May 22, 2010.

11. José de Córdoba and David Luhnow, "In Mexico, Death Toll in Drug War Hits Record," *Wall Street Journal*, January 13, 2011; Jorge Ramos Perez, "La Lucha anticrimen deja 34 mil muertes en 4 años [Anti-crime struggle leaves 34,000 deaths in 4 years]," *El Universal*, January 13, 2011. These are the numbers of drug-related homicides reported nationally for each period of Calderón's term:

December 2006	 62	2009	 9,614
2007	 2,826	2010	 15,273
2008	 6,837		

12. Johanna Tuckman, "Mexico Drugs War Murder Data Mapped," *The Guardian*, January 14, 2011.

13. See, for example, Denise Maerker, "Cifra homicidios en guerra a narco, equivocada: Aguilar Camín [Aguilar Camin reports: Number of homicides in war against narco is wrong]," January 6, 2011, http://www.radioformula.com.mx/notas.asp?Idn=149717.

14. The July 2010 estimate from the CIA World Factbook is available at: https://www.cia.gov/library/publications/the-world-factbook/geos/mx.html.

15. Juárez murders continue to climb, and an accurate count of the victims remains elusive. On March 14, 2011, the Chihuahua State attorney general issued new statistics indicating that there had actually been 3,951 murders in Juárez in 2010, an increase of 840 over the 3,111 widely reported in the media at the end

of 2010 and upping the average to nearly 11 murders per day. ("Once homidi-cios diarios en 2010 en Juárez: Fiscalía [Eleven homicides daily in 2010 in Juárez: Attorney General]," *El Universal*, March 14, 2011, http://www.eluniversal.com.mx/notas/751635.html.) It is highly unlikely that a Mexican government entity would inflate such crime statistics, so this higher number is probably the more accurate one. At an estimated population of 1.2 million, the murder rate in Juárez is 329 per 100,000. To compare, Caracas, Venezuela (population 4 million), has a murder rate of 200 per 100,000 and is often cited as the most violent large city in the Americas; New York City's murder rate is 6; Detroit, known for high crime and poverty, has a murder rate of 46. El Paso's murder rate is about 2; it is reported to be the safest city in the United States with a population over 500,000.

16. "A total of 191 soldiers have been killed fighting drug gangs between December 2006 and Aug. 1, 2010, according to a list of names on a wall of a Defense Department anti-narcotics museum. Reporters saw the list Wednesday during a tour of the museum—the first time the government has made the number public. Forty-three of the soldiers killed were officers. Last week, the government said 2,076 police have been killed since December 2006." See Associated Press, "Mexican Mayor Found Dead 3 Days After Kidnapping," *USA Today*, August 18, 2010, http://www.usatoday.com/news/world/2010-08-18-drug-war-mexico_N.htm.

17. CNN–The Situation Room, "Interview with Mexican President Felipe Calderón; Analysis of Special Election Results" (transcript), aired May 19, 2010, http://transcripts.cnn.com/TRANSCRIPTS/1005/19/sitroom.01.html; Silvia Otero, "No investigan 95% de muertes en 'guerra' [95% of 'war' deaths not investigated]," *El Universal*, June 21, 2010, http://www.eluniversal.com.mx/notas/689120.html. "Las autoridades están rebasadas por los hechos, dicen especialistas; el Presidente ha asegurado que 90% de los decesos por lucha antinarco es de la mafia [The authorities are overcome by events, say specialists; the President has assured that 90% of the deaths in the antinarco struggle are mafia]."

18. Julie Watson and Alexandra Olson, "AP Impact: Mexico Justice Means Catch and Release," *El Paso Times*, July 27, 2010; "Llegan a juzgados pocos homicidios [Few homicide cases reach a court]," *El Diario de Juárez*, November 7, 2009; "El 99% de los delitos en Mexico quedan impunes y todavia estan pendientes 400,000 ordenes de arresto [99% of crimes in Mexico go unpunished and there are 400,000 arrest orders pending]," *Europa Press*, [n.d.], http://www.lukor.com/not-mun/america/portada/08121541.htm.

19. Ignacio Alvarado, "Ven 'limpia social,' no narcoguerra ['Social cleansing,' not a drug war]," *El Universal*, October 18, 2010. An English translation was posted to the Frontera-List: http://groups.google.com/group/frontera-list/browse_thread/thread/6baa726b30751b45/8cea4028513aaa5e.

20. "Free Press, Free People" (editorial), *Globe and Mail* (Canada), March 17, 1997, p. A10.

21. "Termina uno de los años mas violentos en la historia de Juárez; denunciados mas de 22 mil delitos; de 134 asesinatos ocurridos, 40 aclarados [One of the most

violent years in Juárez comes to an end; More than 22,000 crimes reported; of 134 murders, 40 are clarified]," *Norte de Ciudad Juárez*, January 2, 1992.

22. El Cora was a narco-boss working in the 1990s. The sicario tells us a little more about him in this book. There are many cartel operatives who never become known in the press. A video of a narco-corrido on YouTube may be about the same man, though it is impossible to be sure; see http://www.youtube.com/watch ?v=Ud1xPovofuQ. I did find one mention in the Mexican press of a man with the nickname "El Cora de Sinaloa," but we do not know if this is the same man the sicario knew; see Juan Veledíaz, "Hostil recibimiento en tierra de nadie [Hostile reception in no man's land]," *El Universal*, December 14, 2006, http://www .eluniversal.com.mx/nacion/146547.html.

23. "Two More Journalists Shot Dead in Continuing Media Bloodshed," Reporters Without Borders, July 12, 2010, http://en.rsf.org/mexico-two-more -journalists-shot-dead-in-12-07-2010,37925.html.

24. Bowden, *Down by the River*, pp. 288–291; "Murder, Money, and Mexico: The Rise and Fall of the Salinas Brothers," PBS *Frontline* documentary, http:// www.pbs.org/wgbh/pages/frontline/shows/mexico/. See also "Family Tree: General Jesus Gutierrez Rebollo," PBS *Frontline*, http://www.pbs.org/wgbh/pages/ frontline/shows/mexico/family/genrebollo.html; and Fazio, "Mexico: The Narco General Case."

25. Susan E. Reed, "Certifiable: Mexico's Corruption, Washington's Indiffer-ence," *The New Republic*, 1997, reprinted at: http://www.pbs.org/wgbh/pages/ frontline/shows/mexico/readings/newrepublic.html; DEA Congressional Testimony, Statement by Donnie Marshall, Drug Enforcement Administration, United States Department of Justice, Before the House Government Reform and Oversight Committee, Regarding International Narcotics Control, March 18, 1998, http:// www.justice.gov/dea/pubs/cngrtest/ct980318.htm.

26. See Internet Movie Database, "Traffic," http://www.imdb.com/title/ tt0181865/synopsis.

27. Adam Thomson, "Mexico Crime Fighters Die in Air Crash," *Financial Times*, November 5, 2008. See also the following obituaries: Jo Tuckman, "Obitu-ary: Jose Luis Santiago Vasconcelos: Mexican Anti-Drugs Prosecutor Whose Life Was Often Threatened," *The Guardian*, November 17, 2008, p. 34; "Juan Camilo Mouriño," *The Times* (London), November 24, 2008, p. 52.

28. William Booth and Nick Miroff, "Mexican Drug Cartel Forces Lawyer's Video Confessions," *Washington Post*, October 30, 2010; Tracy Wilkinson, "Kid-napped Chihuahua Attorney Found Dead," *Los Angeles Times*, November 6, 2010.

29. "Soldados metidos en un broncón [Soldiers involved in a real mess]," *La Po-laka*, December 2, 2010, http://lapolaka.com/2010/12/02/soldados-metidos -en-un-broncon/.

30. The sicario used a word in Spanish that I had never heard before, "*embarrar*." It means to daub with mud or clay or plaster. It can be used in the sense of "slinging mud," but it can also mean to involve a person in something, to bring someone into an affair, or to complicate a situation. The word can also be used to describe the be-havior of birds who gather together in trees to hide when they are being pursued.

THE YOKE

His head is draped in a black veil. He is not a huge man,
but his body fills the space in the room. When he starts
talking, he lifts his hands to the lens of the camera and you
see nothing but these hands. And he says:

I want to tell you
twenty years of my life,
twenty years of my life
serving narco-trafficking,
serving the cartel,
serving the patron,
with these hands.

Serving them through torture,
serving them by executing so many people
with these hands.

And to those who still belong to these groups of *sicarios*
to those who are still with the cartel,

to those who live in *el chaca**

with the narco . . .

In the world of the cartels,
El chaca is the boss,
the *patron*,
The one who commands, who gives the orders,
And to live *en el chaca*
is to be the one
who guards the boss twenty-four hours a day
with only one day off every seven days.
And since this guard knows everything about the boss
and he also knows what the boss knows,
then he also must be watched twenty-four hours a day.

This is how things are in the lower worlds of the cartels.

But I want to tell you
that you can live in happiness,
that you can throw off the yoke that burdens you
inside the cartel. . . .

---

* Later I asked him to explain *el chaca*, and this is what he wrote:
EL SIGNIFICADO DE ESTA PALABRA EN EL AMBITO DE GRUPOS DE CARTELES SE
LES DENOMINA CHACAS O CHACALOSOS A LOS
JEFES
PATRONES
QUIEN MANDA
QUIEN ORDENA
EL QUE ESTA A CARGO
(*In the cartel world*, el chaca *or* los chacalosos *are words to describe*
the bosses,
the patrones,
those who command,
those who give the orders,
those who are in charge.)

THE
PACKAGE

The door opens, then closes.

I remember clearly that I closed the windows and the curtains.

Okay, good, I thought, that gets rid of a lot of the light. Well, there is still enough light.

"Hey!" I called to my buddies. "Come on in. Bring the guy in here. It's secure."

They came in. We locked the door. The boys were kicking him around.

"Quiet. Calm down. Turn off the light."

And I turned it off.

"Hey! Look. Get down on your knees right there. Kneel down! Listen!"

When he was finally on his knees, I talked to him.

"We are not going to hurt you. We are going to put you in handcuffs. We are going to gag you and blindfold you. This is for your own good and for our benefit also. Put your hands behind you."

So he put his hands behind his back, and I put the handcuffs on him.

"The order is not to hurt you. The only thing that you are going to do, what we want you to do, is pay back the money that you spent. The money that did not belong to you. So, one way or another, you are going to do it. Right now, we are going to wait for orders. And you are going to do whatever we tell you to do.

"Understand? Now, stand up."

He struggled. So we stood him up. And we brought him into the bathroom and ran the water. He might have thought he was going to be comfortable, but no. We put him in the bathtub.

"That is where you will stay. If we hear noise or if you make the least little noise, things are going to go bad for you. And you know what it means when we say things will be bad. . . . We want you calm. We are going to wait for orders. You understand?"

He just moved his head. He could not talk. We closed the door.

I told the other guys: "Hey, turn on the TV. Let's listen to some music. Turn it up loud, so if he makes any noise, no one will hear it.

"Bring some beer. Get out the cocaine, *el perico*, some cigarettes. Everything is okay."

I remember that the boys went out and got some beer.

Ten or fifteen minutes go by. The phone rings.

"Yes, sir, what are your orders? Is everything all right? Yes, sir, everything is fine. He is here and safe. What should we do with him? Yes, sir. Fine. He will call."

So they bring the secure telephone. He is going to make the call. We go and talk to him in the bathroom, we get him out of the tub.

"Hey! Stand up. Stand up."

We bring him over here and sit him on the bed.

"You are going to make a call to your family, and you are going to tell them you are okay. You will tell them that they will get a call and they will be given instructions about where to bring the money, and what's more important, you will let them know they have to pay attention, because if they don't, things are going to be bad. But if everything goes okay, if they deliver what they are supposed to deliver, nothing will happen to you. Talk to them and tell them that you are all right.

"Okay? You understand? I'm going to let you go now."

I cuff his hands in front instead of behind his back, dial the number, and give him the phone.

Instead of talking, he starts to laugh.

I hang up.

"Hey. He doesn't seem to get it," I tell the other guys. "He doesn't want to understand. Look at him laughing."

They say, "Really?"

I tell him, "So is this what you want?"

Then I turn on the water. We fill the tub about half full of water and give him a little therapy.

"Come over here. Are you gonna talk?"

We dunk his head.

"*Ugh. Ugh.*"

"Are you gonna talk?"

After three times under the water, he decided he would make the call. He sat down, I dialed the number for him. And he did what he was told to do. Okay. And after that, he lay back down in the tub, and we turned off the water. Told him not to make noise, and we closed the door.

And so, while we were waiting for more instructions, we stayed there another whole day, sitting around, drinking. . . . Sometimes it was necessary to go into the bathroom, but we were always really careful to keep things very quiet, not to make any noise. We left the door closed because any noise could be heard from inside the bathroom. We had to be very attentive, very careful. The next morning, when the maid came to clean the room, we met her outside the door and just gave her some money. "Don't worry. We will clean the room ourselves. We don't need anything."

• • •

The next morning we knew that we had to give this guy a reason to trust us, to build up his confidence. Make him trust us a little. So we went into the bathroom.

"So, hey, good morning. How are you feeling? Okay? So, how do you like your eggs? Well, all we brought you are boiled eggs. Here. Stand up. Have something to eat."

We put his hands in front, gave him an egg to eat and a glass of water. I brought him over—he was kind of limping from the roughing up we gave him—and I sat with him for a few minutes here in front of the mirror. He was handcuffed.

He sighs and his voice gets soft.

He asked me: "Did they deliver the money?"

"I think so."

"Is everything all right? Are you gonna let me go?"

"Yes, yes, if everything comes out okay, we are going to let you go. You did a bad thing to spend money that did not belong to you. It was a mistake to try to make a fool out of the boss. You know that no one, no one can outsmart the boss."

"But I'm going to pay. I'm going to pay."

"Well, better to say that your family is going to pay. That's more like it. I sure hope that they do not go to the police. Remember, remember, you know the boss finds out everything. Everything. If they go to the police, things will turn out very, very bad for you."

"No, no, they will not tell anyone. They know what will happen to me if they do."

"Okay, you want to lie down here on the bed for a while?"

"Yes, if you will let me."

"Yes."

"Okay."

I brought him over, and he slept there for two or three hours, over here on this side. And we kept on having our little *pachanga,* our little party, with the booze and coke. When he woke up, he moved too quickly and made noise and startled us when he jumped up. We had to knock him around a little.

"Who told you to get up? Now, you lie there and shut up, or we will have to put you back in the bathroom!"

"No, no, no!"

So we put the gag back on him. And while we were doing this we got another call.

The guy who answers tells me, "Here, they want to talk to you," and hands me the phone.

"Yes, what happened? What are the orders, sir? How are we doing? Yes, yes, Okay, I understand. Everything is all right. No, no, no. He's recovering. He's fine. He's okay. Don't worry. Okay."

I tell the guys to bring the phone over here. And I talk to the guy again.

"Look, your family is trying to be smart. They only delivered half the money. We need you to turn over *all* of the money. We know that there is no more money in your bank accounts, but we know that you have some property—some ranches with land and some houses. We need you to call and while you are here in the room with us you will arrange to put these properties in the hands of another person, a real estate agent, and he is going to sell the property while you are here, and once the money is delivered, then we will let you go."

"But you aren't going to do anything to me?"

"Look, just deliver *all* the money. You understand? We are not kidding."

Then we beat him.

"Look! Why didn't your family turn over all of the money if you had it in the bank?"

"No, no, I don't have it. I spent it. . . ."

"Give him a good kicking. Beat him. . . . No, no, never mind. Let him recover. Look, I am going to let you rest on the bed. Trust me."

"Oh, thank you, thank you. You are such a good person. When I get out of here I am going to give you a car. You are behaving really kindly toward me."

"Come on over here. Lie down, make yourself comfortable. Would you like a beer?"

"Uh-uh."

"*Ha!* Are you crazy? You think I'm going to give you a beer? As if. I'm going to give you a glass of water. Here, you want a glass of water?"

"Yes."

"Water is all you are going to get. You want another egg?"

"Yes."

"That's all you are gonna get to eat.

"Okay, now lie down. If you want to get up, you have to let us know. The way to let us know is like this, quietly and calmly: 'Sir, may I get up now?' You ask, and then you wait for my order, to give you permission. If you insist on making noise and getting up again so abruptly, *the boys are gonna put you back in the water!*"

"Yes, sir."

"Okay."

• • •

He managed to get through that day.

At night: "Get up, please. You are going to be able to rest again in your bed. Stay there. Do not make any noise. They have not called, it seems everything is all right. We are going to wait some more."

The other guys start to ask: "What's happening?"

"Nothing, they haven't called."

"Why don't you find out? Are we going to have to pay another day in this hotel or what?"

"Okay. Give me the phone, I'll call."

"Sir—what shall we do? What are the orders? . . . Okay, we will wait another day."

The next morning we are sitting here, very early, about seven forty-five in the morning, I remember. Just a few minutes before eight. The phone rings, and it is the boss's telephone number.

"Yes, what are the orders? Yes, sir. Everything is fine. He is here, he is all right. No, no, no. Everything is okay. Where do you want him? . . . Immediately. Yes, sir. In just a little while. We are close to the bridge. Very close. Okay."

So I tell the other guys: "We are going to let him go. We are going to let him bathe and dress and change and get straightened up. We have to deliver him to the other side. We have to take him over there."

So I told him: "Now everything is okay. Get ready. I'm going to take off the handcuffs. What size shoes do you need? Size nine? Okay."

I tell the guys, "So go get him some pants and a new sweatshirt. Get a razor. Some tennis shoes, size nine. Make sure to bring him that razor too."

"We are going to let you go now. And we want you to look good and feel good. So take a shower and clean yourself up."

They brought the pants, shoes—size nine, the razor. And the guy bathed really quickly, shaved, dressed, and straightened himself up.

The guy was really happy. He didn't look bad, no swelling. The thing with the water was nothing really. The beating he got wasn't so bad.

"Let's go."

We let him feel safe. What did we do? We put him in the backseat of the car. I got in on his right side, he sat in the middle, and another guy on the left side and another guy driving. And we crossed the bridge, and we delivered him to some coworkers there. And from that moment, I never knew anything more about him. And that never mattered to me. It never interested me.

Once the package was delivered, I never tried to find out what happened. That was not my job. My job was done when the package was delivered. You see, once I delivered the package, that was the end of it. That is what I did, and like I told you, I always did a good job. If something bad happened after that, it was because of some mistake the man had made.

And he would have to pay.

✴ CHILD

He sits in room 164 and he says, "These are the four stages of my
life: My childhood, my adolescence, where I formed myself . . . then
I grew into a man, and finally, my salvation in Christ."
He draws the four stages in a black notebook:

CHILD / TEENAGER / MAN / CHILD OF GOD

"We can begin with my childhood. . . ."
And with the word childhood, the voice goes soft. Perhaps
it is the black net veil over his face. He speaks inside of
himself, to himself. A sigh—Oh—marks a memory that
comes sometimes with a smile and often with a sob.
He speaks for two days.
He never stumbles.

He knows the way home.

These are the four stages of my life: My childhood, my adolescence, where I formed myself . . . then I grew into a man, and finally, my salvation in Christ. We can begin with my childhood.

As a little kid, I was a common, ordinary child. My parents didn't have the resources to send us to a good school. We were a large family, a lot of kids. We lived in really small rooms, all of us kids sleeping together on the floor. Thanks to the work that my father and mother did, we never, ever lacked for food. One way or another, by asking for help and through hard work, my parents always found the way to give us the food we needed.

There's an experience I had that I remember well. I was in primary school, maybe third or fourth grade, and this older kid beat up my brother. My brother was older than me. He was in sixth grade at the time. It made me so mad that I started looking for revenge. I waited for this kid outside the school, and I beat him up. This was not a good idea. Yeah, I hit him a few times all right, but he hit me back pretty bad. This caused a lot of bitterness inside of me. And I was traumatized that I was not able to defend myself.

The school called my parents. My mother, like any good mother, went as summoned to see the director of the school. And he told her what had happened. And she accepted it and kept it to herself and only scolded me a little because, well, because she understood that I had been defending my older brother.

Oh, my older brother got so angry with me that he stopped talking to me for months because it made things go really bad for him in school . . . kids saying that he wasn't able to defend himself, that I, his little brother, had to defend him. And so the other kids started treating him like he was a nobody. And even though my mother was called in to see the school director, she never

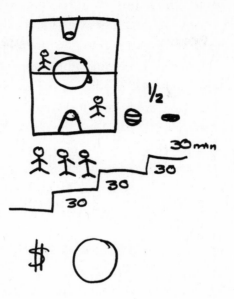

really punished me. She felt proud that I had defended my brother, even though he was older than me.

Back in my childhood, when we had the chance, we would go out to play basketball. I remember we had to play a fast game because the basketball we had was damaged. It had a tiny hole in it and leaked air. It cost us a peso to fill it up, but it would only last about a half hour. And my friends and I would go out onto the court. This was the half hour we had for our game. It was a good time, even if it only lasted thirty minutes. It was fun to be out there on the court, entertaining ourselves, tossing around that old basketball.

And when I think of those thirty minutes when we could play with the basketball . . . when I look back on it now, I realize it is like watching the time pass, and it makes me think about how I grew up. I reflect back on my life, and it was a life lived fast in a very fast world. Those thirty minutes were so short and went by so quickly, just as I feel that I grew up too quickly and my life has passed by too fast. Instead of thinking carefully and following through on the decision to become a professional, to go to the university, to finish a degree, to advance step by step . . . I made decisions on the spot, thirty-minute decisions, just like that thirty-minute ball game. When I left the university and turned my back on a real career, I made that decision in thirty minutes, and after that I always looked for the fastest way to get the things that I wanted—money, drugs, power. Fast, easy things.

• • •

Some years went by. I continued my education. I always got good grades in school. And I won some scholarships and half-scholarships, and this served me well, but I kept having this resentment inside of me from this feeling of powerlessness, that I could not have a car. Because at the next higher level after primary school, I could see the kids with their cars, how they could go out, go to the movies, have fun. . . .

All of this time I was living through, growing up, I kept thinking and having the idea that I could be somebody. Somebody big, somebody with power. Somebody who could say something and make it happen. Somebody with no limits. A person who could say, "I want that." And have it. A person who could have a craving for something to eat, and have it. I wanted to be the man who could wish for a really big house, and have it.

I was very young, but I had these big desires. They were not really good desires, but they were big and they were real. I wanted to have all of this quickly, and I was always looking for the fastest and easiest way to get what I wanted.

• • •

Oh, when I think back on my parents, I remember that all they did was work, work, and more work. There was not much of a relationship between my parents and their children. I didn't know anything about going to the theater or the movies because my parents just did not have the money for us to learn about those things.

The only time—and I remember it well, and will always carry this memory with me—we did something together was when a circus came to town and somehow my parents found a way to take me and two of my younger brothers to the circus. But they told us there was one condition: Once we were there, we could not ask for anything else because there was only enough money for the tickets to get in. So, because of this situation, and knowing that we would get hungry while the show was on and ask for food or treats, my mother prepared some food to take along.

She got some *Galletas Marias*—cookies that were very common in Mexico—and some *mole* sauce, and she made us sandwiches with the mole and the cookies. So that once we were there and enjoying the circus, my father would have just enough money to buy two sodas that we could all share. But I remember that the mole spilled and the cookies got smashed and stuck to the paper napkins they were wrapped in, but it didn't matter to us. It didn't matter to us at all. . . .

The voice breaks. He tells the rest of the story
through tears, the joy of that moment and the sadness
of his only memory of an outing with his father.

On that day my brothers and I were really happy, happier than we had ever been. We had never ever been taken out anywhere with my father before, and had never known what it was to go out to the circus. We never knew what it was to have fun. We had always envied other kids for the things they had that we didn't have. But in this moment we felt so proud to enjoy eating those cookies and mole, even though we had to eat the paper napkins too. I thanked my father over and over for this fun that he gave us, for the sacrifice that he made. It might have cost him a week or more of food for the family to take us to the circus, but it made me the happiest kid in the world.

And for years after that day, whenever my brothers and I see each other, even when we haven't been together for a long time, this is the first thing we talk about and remember.

"You remember when we went to the circus?"

"Remember how we ate those cookies with mole?"

"Remember how our dad had to get a few cents more to buy those two sodas?"

"Remember how happy we were?"

In that moment we didn't need or want anything else. And I learned who my father was. From my point of view, I had always felt that it was unfair that the only thing my father did was work, work, and work some more. All he ever wanted to do was teach us how to work.

"Get to work and make some cement, make some blocks, so we can build some more rooms on the house," he'd say.

I wanted to have fun, but for my father, having fun was putting us to work. That day that he took us to the circus, I don't know if he got a little extra money or what. But for my whole life, I will thank him for this. It was a moment that marked our childhood and brought us together as brothers.

My younger brothers and I were always fighting over things. If one of us got some new socks, the others had to wait until the older ones outgrew the socks so the littler ones could use them. Once I got to wear something, the younger ones had to wait. The littlest had to wait so long that everything was worn out by the time it got to him. And it was the same with underwear, pants, all of our clothes. It was like a staircase. Our parents would buy stuff for the older ones and then it got passed down to all the others.

Oh, but that day we went to the circus was fascinating. On that day the three of us were equal. We all ate the same thing. We all had fun. And for years and years we all remember it as the best thing that ever happened to us in our childhood. It is something that I feel is so much mine, something that belongs to me. And when my brothers and I meet now and talk about it, we all start to cry, because not one of us ever had any idea where my father got the money to buy those circus tickets.

• • •

I often think about Sundays. On Sunday, everybody in the *colonia,* neighborhood, would run out to buy their snow cones or popsicles or candy because everybody would get a little money to spend on Sundays. I didn't know what Sunday was all about, just that since it was Sunday, we had to go to Mass and leave an offering for the poor. In our family we never knew anything about getting money to spend on Sunday until one time I remember when my father got a little better job and my mother also had started to work cleaning houses. And after that they were able to give us five or ten cents to spend.

Oh, *wow!* That was really something! Ten cents to spend on Sunday!

"Let's all go to the store to buy candy."

So five of us brothers and sisters would get together and buy one big bag of candy. Or we would buy a big pack of popcorn and divide it up and count out the pieces of popcorn so we could make it last four days. We would count it out so that we each had twenty pieces of popcorn every day. And on the day we would borrow or rent a TV (we didn't have a TV, so we would pay a peso to go and watch TV at a neighbor's house) we would bring our own popcorn.

Every Monday we would gather together and watch a really famous program in Mexico, *El Chavo del Ocho*. And each of us would bring their twenty pieces of popcorn. This was just on Monday, that's when the program was on.

TEENAGER

I kept growing . . . I changed schools. I developed other interests. Some of the other kids now had cars, but I always had to take the bus. To go from the house to the school, I had to pay, and sometimes I had to walk 'cause I didn't have money for the bus, and it could be hard to ask for a ride. But at this time, the city of Juárez was still pretty friendly. There were not many bad feelings among the people, it was easy to ask for a lift, and people would often give rides to school kids with their backpacks.

At high school I made some new friends, but I had an itch. I kept wanting to better myself, to get more things, to be more, to have more things like the other kids had. But for me and my parents, it was hard. And so some of us chose an easier path.

When we were in secondary school, a person invited us to a party, and he showed us how nice things could be. He made us see that we could drink and have fun, and what's more, that we could have money and maybe even a car.

So I asked this guy, "Okay, how? What do I have to do?"

And he says, "Nothing, just drive this car to your school and deliver it to me in the morning. When you leave school in the afternoon, you will drive it over to El Paso and deliver it to me there."

"And then?"

"After that, I'll give you another car, you can use it all week, I'll fill it up with gas for you. And on the weekend you give it back to me, and then you take it to El Paso for me, and then I'll loan you another car and I'll pay you."

"Is that all?"

"No, that's not all. Here you've got a house that you can use. There will be girls who can help you out and serve your needs. You'll like it. You can even live here if you like."

Ah, at this time, there were four of us guys who said, sure, yeah. My mother missed me a lot 'cause I hardly ever went home. I didn't even know how to drive, but in one day someone taught me to drive a car. I didn't have a license, but in half an hour some-one got a license for me.

Oh, I remember one of the things that happened at that time. I was crossing over to the United States, and I was driving a big car with Colorado plates. And I got stopped on the bridge.

The immigration guys asked me who the car belonged to, and I said, "A friend."

"And why are you driving it?"

"Because they loaned it to me."

"Do you have a license?"

"Yes."

"Do you have money?"

"Of course."

"And what do you do?"

"I'm a student."

"And why do you have money?"

"Because I work."

"What do you do?"

"Oh, I clean motel rooms."

"Where?"

"In Mexico."

"Okay."

They took my passport and put it in front of the window and told me to go into a cubicle. When I stood up, they told me to sit down by an iron bar. So I sat down, and a person came with a little dog and opened the trunk of the car, and the dog started to go crazy, barking. When this happened, wow, before I could even turn around, there were like six people surrounding me and on top of me already.

I said, "Hey, what's going on? Far as I know, I'm not carrying anything."

"Okay."

They put me in a little room with bunk beds in it, just one door and one window and a glass I couldn't see through. Maybe they could see me. I don't know. I couldn't see them.

The guy says to me, "You are gonna have to take off all your clothes, put all your things here. We are going to search you."

"Why?" I asked.

"It's possible that you are carrying drugs in the car."

"No, that's not true."

"Good. We are going to search you. Take off your clothes."

So they took off all my clothes. Took everything out of my wallet. They looked at every piece of paper I was carrying. For three hours they asked me about every bit of information in my wallet.

"Who is this number for? Who is this person that you know?"

I was carrying a bunch of cards with American phone numbers, and they asked me about every one of those phone numbers. Suddenly I see the guy with the dog come into the office. I'm not sure what they were saying in English.

But the guy told me, "Okay, put your things away."

"Okay."

They had already let me put on my clothes, and so I put all my stuff away. And they put a paper in front of me. "Here, take this."

"Well, what's this for?" I asked.

They said, "So, look here. You have to sign and say that we did not treat you badly, that we were just doing our job. That we never did anything bad to you. And we are going to let you go and you won't have any problems."

"Well, tell me what happened then. Why all this trouble?"

And he said, "Look, we have a dog that detected that you were carrying drugs in the car. So when we put your car up on a ramp and looked under it, we saw that the screws on the gas tank had been moved around. Did you work on this car, change those screws around?"

"No." I told them that the car was borrowed, that I never worked on it. "I'm not a mechanic. I'm just a student who works. I came over to have some fun."

I remember real well that time, that I had just enough money to buy a pizza. For us to buy a pizza at Peter Piper Pizza in El Paso was a big deal—*lo maximo!* There wasn't any such thing as Peter Piper Pizza in Mexico then. If we went over there to buy pizza, it meant we had some real money!

"Okay, well, I'm not going to sign," I said. "I want to talk to my lawyer."

Oh, man, they really got angry with me when I said that. They made some bad faces at me and said they were not going to give me back my border-crossing card, my *mica*.

Well, when they said that, I realized that without the *mica* I would not be able to use the cars or get the fifty dollars every week. I wouldn't be able to give rides to girls. Lots of things I wouldn't be able to do. But then they ended up giving it back to me anyway.*

• • •

Of all the many things that I did, the one that I always enjoyed the best was, when I got the fifty dollars, I would take out twenty dollars and put it aside for my mother. She would go out to buy things for the family every two weeks when she got paid, and so I would say to her, "Here, take this twenty dollars."

She was always so happy and would ask me where I got the money. "Working!" I would tell her that I got it going to El Paso to do yard work.

My mother was really happy. She never knew what I was actually doing to get the money. I never knew what the drugs were that I carried. I knew the cars I drove over the bridge were loaded, but I didn't know with what, or how much exactly, or where the drugs were hidden. When they told me that stuff about the gas

---

* More than a year after the initial interview, the sicario told us in a casual conversation that a U.S. official who worked in a border agency at the time (probably in the late 1980s) had helped get his border-crossing card back after this incident when he was caught at the bridge. Years later, the sicario said, he lost the card again during a cocaine-snorting party on the U.S. side of the border. The same official intervened again, the implication being that the drug traffickers the sicario worked for at the time had connections inside U.S. agencies.

tank, I figured that's where the drugs were, but I never really knew. So during those three years, me and three other guys lived off of this, and that's how we got through secondary school.

It was a happy time. I did not depend on my parents. I would give them money when I could. I bought my own clothes, my own Converse tennis shoes. Man, I remember the time I bought some Reeboks. Wow! They cost eighty dollars. I was the only one in my school with Reeboks. I bought them at JCPenney's. The other kids were jealous, and they would tease me and step on my shoes, just to piss me off. It made me really mad.

Some of my other friends were less ostentatious. They had done this for a longer time. I only did it every two weeks or so. It was rare that I did it every week. Some of them did it three times per week. My parents were more conservative, and I didn't have permission to spend too much time away from home. I couldn't get away from the house as much.

I studied hard, earned really good grades, and I was automatically accepted into preparatory school. It wasn't the best school in Juárez, but it was a pretty good school. Once in prep school, you have to have your car, a good body, play American football, go to the gym a lot, and have some money to spend. That was the way to get girlfriends. I could usually have one or two girlfriends, no problem. While at prep school, I quit working for those people for a while because I got a scholarship and had to spend all my time studying and playing sports. The scholarship paid me just a small sum of money.

So what I did was use the little bit of money that I had saved from the three years I had been working and bought an old car. I also started working in another, legal business. But in this business, I ran into a kind of vicious circle. I always found that there were some really good people, some others who were more or less good, and then there were the bad people. The bad people liked to hang out in the bars and cantinas and take drugs. At that time I found myself right here in the middle. But unfortunately, *desgraciadamente*, I made the choice to get in with the bad people.

He illustrates the vicious circle in a drawing.

I started to help them out some. And I started using drugs. We didn't use marijuana much. And it was hard to get cocaine at this time. If we wanted cocaine, we would have to send someone to El Paso, Texas, to get it and bring it back to Juárez. At that time, if anyone had cocaine, it meant they had a lot of money.*

Back then in Juárez, not many drugs were for sale. I know that Juárez is and always was a bridge to pass drugs into the U.S., but at that time the drugs weren't sold here in Juárez. It was forbidden to open the shipments of cocaine in Juárez. The drugs arrived here and were passed into the United States, but in Juárez they were not for sale. A little marijuana, yes, but not cocaine. And heroin had been around for a long time. In the past I had never liked marijuana or heroin. Once in secondary school, I smoked marijuana a little, but it made me sick and I vomited for two days. It was later, in prep school, and gradually when I got involved with the bad people and went to a lot of parties, that I started to use cocaine.

• • •

So what happened? In this time period, a gram of cocaine cost $120. You had to get $120 to get a gram of cocaine. That would

---

* From the early 1990s until after the death of Amado Carrillo in 1997, the cartel forbade the sale of nearly all illegal drugs in the city of Juárez. This was part of an arrangement between the Juárez cartel and the government. This control broke down after Carrillo's death. The domestic drug market is now an important part of the business in Juárez and all over Mexico.

be thirty dollars each for the four of us. You had to work to get that, but it wasn't much, it was never enough. Our consumption between the four of us was a lot more than a gram. Now, you are talking about *un ocho*. This was twenty-eight grams of cocaine. That's what we would have to buy to supply us for several days of partying.

We would still get good grades in school. Being young, we were in really good shape. We could run, our bodies responded. Being drugged (on cocaine) I think made it easier to withstand getting injured playing American football and other sports. I guess I could have had a heart attack or something, but thank goodness that never happened.

A lot of times I went to school really high or really drunk. We would drink all night and in the morning put on our uniforms and go to school. My parents never realized what was going on. My father had a night-shift job. He worked all night and would get home at six o'clock in the morning and sleep till six o'clock at night. So he never knew what I did all day. Much less what I did all night.

So what happened then? My mother was out working cleaning houses. When she was doing this, she would work Monday to Friday away from home and would only come back to our house on Saturday and Sunday. She worked like this so that we would have plenty to eat and be able to pay for our schooling.

Oh, school for me was never a problem. You know, I think that if I had just kept studying, I could have been a good engineer or architect or doctor or something. I got good grades without even trying. I never remember studying for a test. I would take a few classes, read the book for an hour before the test, and then show up for the exam, and I never got a score of 7 (or lower). I would always get an 8 or 9 or 9.8 or an 8, but never a 7 or a bad grade.

Sometimes if I didn't know the material on the test, it wouldn't matter because I always had some money. I would sit next to some other kid who knew the stuff who would fill out the exam but leave the name blank. Then he would give me his test all filled out, and I'd put my name on it, turn it in, and give him the money. And my blank exam. It was easy for me because I never had any trouble getting money.

So I didn't have any problems. But it was while I was in prep school that we got to know another kind of people. These people made a proposition to us to sell drugs in the school. Oh, I couldn't do very well at this, because I was on two teams—American football and basketball. I didn't have much time, and since I had scholarships to play sports, I got paid a little bit from that. But what these people did was pay me for access to my lockers. I had two lockers with keys, and in one of them I would store some drugs for them and put my stuff in the other one. But I always had to be very careful and keep watch so that no one opened the locker with the drugs. We had to get into the school sometimes at night to get the drugs from the lockers to sell to those who wanted them.

For me it was really emotional. It wasn't hard for me. Everything at this time was full of emotion for me. To be sixteen years old and to be able to live like this! To have money and to be able to invite any girl I wanted to go out to eat in nice restaurants with me. And I always had enough that I could invite two friends to go along. I could tell the mariachis to play any song I wanted to hear. "Hey, babe! Play 'La Muchacha Alegre,' play 'El Rey.' How much? Here, let me pay you."

There weren't many kids who had the money to do this. And we were just imitating the people who *really* had the money to live this kind of life. We never realized that this money that we were spending so fast could have done us a lot of good tomorrow, if we had saved some for the future. This money—oh, we really spent it badly—but it was such a happy time for us. But then, sometimes after a few days, we wouldn't have any money left, not even enough to buy gas. And so I would ask those who were paying us for a loan. And they would say, "Okay, sure, how much do you need?"

"Well, this much."

"Okay. But to get the loan, you will have to make a run to El Paso."

I know it was an abuse they were committing, that they were taking advantage of us. When I started doing it, they would only pay me fifty dollars to cross a car. I never knew what was in that car that I was crossing or how much. So I would ask them for more money. "Look, I need at least a hundred dollars."

And then one day they said, "We are not going to give you one hundred dollars, we are going to give you a *thousand* dollars. But the car is already parked near the bridge. The person who was going to do it got very nervous, and now he is too afraid to cross it. You want the thousand dollars?"

"Hell, yeah, of course I want it."

So I went to get the car, got in, and I crossed it. And while I was crossing, I remember very well, two cars followed me all the way to the apartments where I was supposed to deliver it in El Paso. I went to the place where I was told to leave the car, got out, put the keys where I had been told, went into the apartment where my contact was, and collected an envelope with one thousand dollars. And that was the last time I ever saw those people.

I later found out that the person who had chickened out on this job was the same man who had recruited me for this work back when I was in secondary school. And he had become afraid because the same thing that had happened to me at the bridge that one time (being stopped and searched) had happened to him twice in a row. He thought it wasn't safe anymore, that people were being checked, and that the cars we used had been identified.

This didn't matter very much to me. I needed money. I did not give all of it to my mother for the household for sure. I spent a lot of it on myself and having fun. What I really liked was being the most famous kid in the school. To be the one who would go to the cafeteria with six or seven friends and all of our girl-friends too, and I would tell them to get whatever they wanted and I would pick up the tab. I liked it because when I played sports, I'd have a whole lot of fans. They would all know that after the game I'd buy them a lot of beers or invite them all to a bar on me. It felt really good.

It was about this time—when I was sixteen—when I got into my first dance hall. I remember that the guy at the door said, "You are a minor. I can't let you go in." But I handed him a fifty-dollar bill, and he said, "Okay, no problem. . . ." And so I went into my first dance hall. I didn't know how to dance, but I knew how to drink a lot, and I got along real well with all the waiters.

It was splendid! I would drink two or three pitchers of beer, maybe twenty-five dollars worth, and then I'd leave a thirty-dollar tip, more than the cost of the drinks I bought. And the waiters would really like that. I would sometimes bring a group of friends, and they would treat me really special. "Ah, señor, come in, come in. We have a table ready for you." That was the best time of all. I learned the power of having money, that with money I could do anything. The saying at the time was, "With money, you can make the dog dance. Without money you dance like a dog."

But life got a little worse for us. My mother got sick, and her health soon got so bad she couldn't work anymore. She kept get-ting sicker. And I made my decision to go to the university and leave all of my vices behind. And that is how it was. Part of what was happening with my mother was because. . . . Well, all mothers have a way of knowing what is going on with each one of their children. They might not say anything, but they sense it. My mother knew I was the black sheep of the family. She was always worrying about me. I noticed that when all my brothers and sisters did things wrong, she would scold them and correct them, but the only things she ever said to me were: "Be careful." "Behave yourself." "Try to do the right thing." "Trust in God to take care of you." "Do the right thing."

She always seemed very concerned about me. Whenever I wasn't going to come home for a few days, I would call from a pay phone (there weren't any cell phones then) to a neighbor's house to tell my mother that I was going to spend the night with friends, not to worry, that I was going to school, but just not coming home for a few days.

I found out later that my mother would cry a lot when this happened. She didn't know what I was doing or if I was okay, or where I was. She worried so much about me that one day we held a family meeting. My oldest sister called the meeting, and she was going to do the talking. We were all there at the table, about thirteen of us—we were a big family—we all found our places there at this big table.

He draws the round table and sketches in all the family members.

My oldest half-sister (she was the daughter of my mother but had a different father) had called the meeting of the family. And all of my brothers and sisters ganged up on me and told me that it was my fault that my mother was sick. They said things like:

"My mother is sick because of you."

"My mother is sick because you don't come home."

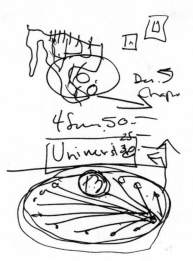

"My mother is sick because she knows what you are up to."

"My mother is sick because of you drinking and doing drugs. . . ."

The last to speak was the eldest, my half-sister. She said, "You all have always thought of me as the oldest, but as separate from this family. You know, I only have a mother. She is my mother. Your father is not my father. I just have my mother, and I love her very much, and I want to protect her and enjoy her. And I can tell you this. If you want to keep on like you are, it would be better for you to just disappear from this family and we'll say you are dead. I have no other family except my mother. You either have to straighten up and behave yourself or we are going to send you to join the army."

Oooooh. I laughed at that. *Ha!*

So I said, "Yeah, right. You *think* you are going to send me to the army. As if! Don't you worry about me. I am going to fix everything."

• • •

It took me two days. I was in my fourth semester at the university when this happened. In two days, thanks to recommendations from some friends and acquaintances [people he had met from his drug-smuggling activities], I arranged to get started on my career in the police. There were several requirements to joining the police that you had to fulfill. First, you had to be of majority age of eighteen. Second, you had to have a draft card, and to get that you had to be of age. Third, almost always, you had to be married. Fourth, you had to pass a drug test, and fifth, a physical exam. I was not of majority age, nor did I have my draft card. I could not pass the drug test. I wasn't married. The only thing I could pass of all these requirements was the physical examination.

When I had my interview with the head of the academy, he said, "There are just two problems that will keep you out of the academy. But since you come with very good recommendations, this is not going to be a problem. But you have to do me a favor. You need to stop using drugs. Not being married is not going to be a problem. You don't have your draft card, but I'm going to send you to the military headquarters, and you will talk to a specific person there, and he will give you the card that you need."

I said, "No. I don't have to, because the person who sent me here to you said that you were going to accept me without any papers. You want me to call him and tell him that you are asking for this?"

Then he said, "Okay, never mind, get out of here. Go and report to so-and-so. Bring a couple of changes of clothes, shorts, tennis shoes."

And that is how I began my career in the police academy.

✳

MAN

I had gotten two big breaks. So now—after all of my family had rejected me in that meeting organized by my oldest sister, when they told me that I was the worst and that it was my fault that my mother was sick and that no one was going to provide any money for me—after all that, I said, "No problem . . . I'll take care of everything."

I immediately left the university because I didn't have the money to keep studying. I was able to fulfill all of the entrance requirements [with help from some of the powerful people I had been working for], and I enrolled in the police academy and began the training course. I learned to march and then to march some more, how to form up, line up, and stand at attention, how to straighten up and follow orders.

They even taught us how to keep a schedule. If you get up at five forty-five in the morning, by five fifty you have to be showered and finished up in the bathroom and dressed. Once you were lined up in the ranks to salute the flag in the morning, you could not stop and say, "Oh, wait, I have to go to the bathroom." You had to be ready, ready for some tough training.

This training lasted six months. During these six months, one of the tasks I was given [by my mentors in the narco-trafficking organization] was to recruit other people. One of the reasons I advanced rapidly in the police is that people on the U.S. side of the border paid a certain amount of money—that came from the United States—for those who were enrolled in the police training course. In the academy as a cadet, you were paid about half of the salary of an officer who had completed the course and who was now on duty in the police force. But for me, this money was nothing. The money sent to me each month from the American side, from El Paso, now that was real good money. So I had what I needed. They sent me money, drugs, and women.

So what did we do? During the night there were guards there in the academy to keep us in. There are rooms and basketball courts and shooting ranges. A fence and cars parked outside and the guards. We would corrupt the guards with a hundred dollars and a gram of cocaine, just buy them off so they would let us leave the academy at night. We would go out at about 7:00 P.M. and return at five thirty in the morning. Why at five thirty? Because at five forty-five the morning whistle would sound and we would have to get up, and at five fifty we would have to be all lined up for roll call and to salute the flag.

And why were all these cadets recruited? At the time, I didn't completely understand what was going on. For me at this time,

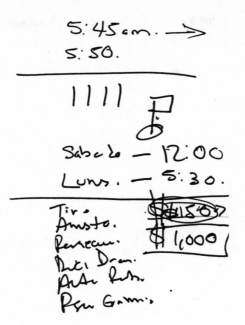

things were really good. I was happy. I had money, cars, drugs. They sent me girls and paid for hotel rooms. On Saturdays we were free to leave at noon and had to be back Monday morning by five thirty at the latest. I was unusual in that I never got arrested or got into any trouble. I was very careful about my schedule. There were schedules for everything: showers, meals, exercise, classes. We took classes in marksmanship, how to make arrests, how to pursue suspects, drug detection, car theft investigation, criminal psychology. . . .

But what was really going on? Why were they teaching me all of this when I was being paid from outside? People connected to the narco-traffickers were paying for me and for others who, sooner or later, would be recruited to work for them. The government officially paid about one hundred and fifty pesos per month, and that was nothing. But these people on the outside were paying us one thousand dollars per month! They knew that when we left the academy we were going to go to work for them. No one was ever going to pay us as much as they, the narco-traffickers, were paying. We were being trained.

• • •

Sadly, *desgraciadamente*, all of the law enforcement academies in Mexico—the different police forces, the investigative police, the military police, and the army—have been used by the narco-trafficking organizations as training grounds for their future employees. Thus, all of those who pass through the academies can easily be recruited by the narcos. Everything taught in these academies—how to use weapons, how to drive a car, how to conduct surveillance, how to read license plates, how to recognize faces, how to pursue people in urban car chases without losing them—all of these were skills that the narco-trafficking organizations were willing to pay a lot of money for. But because the narcos were able to use the official law enforcement academies, they did not have to work very hard to train their operatives. They could just take advantage of the training provided by the government and then recruit cadets like us to do their work.

On Saturdays we would go out. . . . I remember that they would come for me on a red Harley Indian motorcycle and in a car. I would bring four or five cadets along for the ride. "Let's go." We would go to El Paso. The first place we would go was to a downtown store called Starr Western Wear. We would stock up on really good blue jeans, western shirts, big fancy belt buckles. At this time the style was to wear very flashy clothes, to shine, to show we had money and power. Back then, the judicial police were really into fancy boots. The municipal police wore uniforms, but when they went out on the town they would also wear cowboy boots.

After the shopping, we would usually go to an apartment. Not to hotels. We tended to make a lot of noise and did not want to cause scandals in a hotel. A few times we went to a house with a pool. When we arrived, the cartel patrons who were paying our way would say to us, "Here are some girls. They will stay with you until you leave on Sunday night. Choose whichever ones you want."

They would leave us envelopes with money, a rock of cocaine, marijuana, psychotropic pills. They left us everything we could want to have a good time. They wanted us to be contented and happy with them. Always, always, always, they made us feel that we were important to them. They never asked us for much in return at this time. They always wanted to make us happy: with money, drugs, and women. If you needed economic help, they would say, "Here you go. . . ." Everything was available to us. Then we would return to the academy for more training when the weekend was over.

• • •

At the end of our training in the academy, we graduated. On graduation day, a selection process takes place. There are about two hundred men in the graduating class. Two hundred for the whole state of Chihuahua, which is a very large state. Our class of cadets were being trained to police the cities of Juárez, Villa Ahumada, Chihuahua City, Parral, Camargo, Delicias, Ojinaga, and also the state border posts with Durango and Sonora. Of these two hundred graduates, fifty are already on the payroll of the

narco-trafficking organizations. So there are one hundred and fifty men who will be assigned to all of the posts around the state. But of those other fifty who are working for the narcos, twenty-five stay in Juárez, five in Chihuahua City, five in Parral, five in Ojinaga. They are distributed in such a way that when the offer comes to them to pass drugs into Chihuahua from Durango, Sonora, or Coahuila, there are people already on the job at the ports of entry into the state who are committed to working for the narco-trafficking organizations so that the drugs will be able to circulate easily.

Many, many, many times, official police vehicles are used to transport drugs. There were other occasions when it was just a matter of hiding the drugs in a trailer which then passes on through with the blessing of the police. But at this time there was a very important rule in effect: The drugs were never opened in Juárez, ever.

When the tractor-trailer trucks arrived, they would be taken to warehouses to be unloaded. The walls inside the trailer would be broken down. The drugs would be separated out from the other cargo in the trailer, which would then leave. These trailers were used mostly for marijuana and cocaine. Heroin was almost never transported in these trailers. It would come in from Parral or from the countryside in cars. All the fruit that was hauled in these refrigerator trucks—bananas, papayas, other kinds of perishables, sometimes forty tons or more in the various trailers—would be unloaded and given away to the people in poor barrios. We would take it in trucks and deliver it to the people. Meanwhile, others who were part of the narco-trafficking organization would be opening the compartments in the trailers and unloading the drugs, putting them in other vehicles, and then this merchandise would be taken to safe houses.

How many safe houses are there? A lot. So many that one person might only know about eight or ten of them. For instance, I might have personal knowledge of ten houses in Juárez, but I will only know those eight or ten houses. And for example, "El Dos," Number 2, another person, will have another set of safe houses that he is in charge of.

The narco-trafficking organizations are very careful. Each operative only knows certain houses. And the bosses know exactly how many houses each operative knows. The bosses let you know only what they want you to know. Because the day that you try to defraud the organization, they will know who is doing it by where things happen, because they know that you can only expose the houses that you know about.

• • •

When dealing with marijuana. . . . It is incredibly blatant, the way they transport it. They barely make any effort to hide it. They hitch a flatbed trailer to a pickup truck with a tow-bar. The trailer is stacked with boxes of marijuana, and these trucks will travel all over the city as if they were hauling boxes of any other material. We are not talking about one, two, three, or four . . . no, we are talking about thirty, forty, or fifty tons of marijuana that will have to be transported, stored, and guarded.

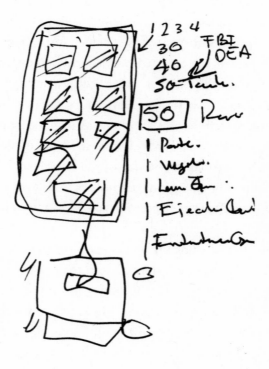

In the recruitment that they carry out in the academy, of the fifty graduates who are actually on the payroll of the narco-trafficking organizations, each has their function in the operation. Some are assigned to guard the safe houses. Others are assigned to keep those guys under surveillance. Another group is assigned to kidnap people who owe money or who have gone to work for another gang or rival group. Others specialize in executing people. And another group is assigned to bury the people who have been executed. All of the functions are separated into these different groups with different assignments.

Why is it arranged this way? This is what I learned, and there's a really good saying that describes it: "Never mix up Christmas with New Year's." For example, if you are assigned to kidnap someone, then you deliver the victim to another person, "El Dos" [*Number 2*], who delivers him to "El Tres" [*Number 3*], who will deliver him to the person who executes him, who then delivers him to the person who buries the body. It would seem like a simple kind of triangulation—that the people who do the kidnapping, interrogating, killing, and burying would be able to figure it all out—but that's not the way the narco-traffickers operate. What they want from this system of exchange in all these functions is to obscure the knowledge of where all of these bodies are buried.

It takes a number of years working for the organization before the director of the cell has enough confidence in you and enough wisdom to say, "Here's what you must do. You kidnap the guy and deliver him to this one and that one, and you wait here until he is buried and that's it."

While he is speaking, he makes a drawing
of the operation he is describing.

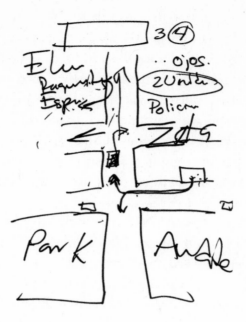

So, for example, here is a street. Here a park, and over here, this is an auditorium. The person who is going to be kidnapped will be watched for three or four days beforehand. For this, two people will be used who are called *ojos*, "the Eyes." They will keep watch on the person's house for several days from different vantage points. They will see exactly when the person comes and goes, where he goes, who he goes out to eat with, and so forth. . . . They will follow his routine, wherever he goes, for a whole week or longer.

These Eyes will be supported by two cars. And these are not private cars, but police cruisers. When an ordinary citizen goes somewhere and sees an official patrol car following him, with its sirens and insignia, the person will never suspect for a moment that he will be kidnapped or disappeared. Because, of course, the police are there to serve the community and protect the community. The police are not there to kidnap people. What this person never suspects is that members of the police force are recruited from their time in the academy, bought and paid for by the narco-traffickers, to carry out specific jobs in the criminal organizations.*

There are two methods used in these operations. After a week of surveillance, noting where the target goes and all of the routes he takes, a team is designated. This team is composed of five vehicles that are stationed at various points around the person's house. The Eyes keep doing their job. On the day that the act will take place, first of all the police are notified to get all of the patrol cars out of this sector. And this notice is not given to the patrolling officers in those cars, but to the director of the police. For instance, someone will call the director and tell him, "We don't want any police in the area for a certain time period." Or they tell the director to call a meeting of police personnel for a certain time, say, ten to ten forty-five. The message will be: "We don't want any police on the street. . . . We are going to work."

The target leaves his house. There are one or two police cars that look identical, but these are not really police cars, and they go to work. They follow the objective, and they stop him. There are times when the target will not stop. Sometimes, if the guy is a real *plebe malandro*, just a very bad dude, and he knows he owes money to the boss and that it is not going to go well for him, he

---

* People who worked for the narco-trafficking organizations would carry out these tasks whether they were on or off police duty. In another interview, the sicario described paying off dispatchers with a few hundred pesos to avoid interruption while partying or while engaged in criminal activities.

will probably not stop for the patrol car. That's why there are five cars stationed around him, like this.

He draws the plan out in a notebook—one, two, three, four, five cars as little blocks, like a football coach diagramming a special play.

The Eyes follow behind. Of all these cars, only one will be used to kill the guy or kidnap him. If the patrol car is not able to get him to stop, the other cars will block his way even if they have to cause a crash in the street. The problem here is how the boss wants the target: alive or dead? If the boss wants him dead, that's easy.

The Eyes move, the second car moves out, the one that stops him stays behind, one closes him off from the front. You never have to worry about crossfire. One car pulls up from the side, shoots him, and that's it. Everyone retreats. In less than three minutes, all five cars are six or seven blocks away guarded in safe houses that are nearby. You just walk away from the scene and get picked up by another vehicle and go to eat at a restaurant nearby, calm and tranquil, as if it were nothing.

Since all the police patrols had been called into a meeting, it takes the police an hour or more to get to the scene. So for more than an hour, the scene of the crime is open to people walking all around, checking out what happened, and messing up the evidence left behind. And there are always some clever folks hanging around who pick the pockets and steal the wallets of the onlookers. This is all part of our strategy.

But there are some cases when the person is wanted alive. And this requires a different strategy.

You have to watch the target very carefully from the time he leaves his house and wait for a suitable place to stop him and force him to get out of the car. When he gets out of his car, you have to immediately get him into your car. Physically, you sense that it is not fear exactly, but adrenaline that rises up in you. It's human nature. . . . And being human, you know that it is not enough to just say to the guy, "Hey, come with me." And expect him to obey.

He isn't going to come. So you get there, and you are going to have to grab him, beat him, handcuff him, and put him in your car by force. But this car is not traveling alone. There are three more cars ahead and another two behind. If an actual police patrol car dares to intervene along the route, one of these cars may have to ram it, and if they still don't get the message, then you may have to shoot up the police car.

That's why these days* the police have been so persecuted and criticized. If they had been given the word back at the time they were in the police academy, that they were being trained to serve a certain person or organization, well, when the time comes and they receive orders from that person who is a boss at some level in the drug-trafficking organization, they know that they have to carry these orders out or they will be killed. This is what is happening now. It is one thing to just tell them to get out of the way. But if they get the order, they have no choice except to *"get the fuck out of the way!"*

• • •

Up until a few years ago, the narcos respected the lives of women and children. But starting sometime in 2008, it seems that this practice of respecting the lives of women and children has been forgotten. Why? Because the narcos started to recruit women to work as debt collectors for them. And those women try to protect themselves by using their children as shields. And so the agreement no longer functions. There is no longer any plan. Before, if a targeted person left his house with a child, as soon as it was known that a child was present, the mission would be aborted. The killing would take place another day when the guy was alone. But now, such agreements have all been terminated.

Where would kidnapped people be taken? Let's say you pick up a person. Take him out of his car, put him in another car. Always, always, the safe house would be no more than five blocks— that is the very farthest that it would be—from the scene of the

---

* The sicario is referring to the current climate of extreme violence that began in January 2008.

kidnapping. The car will pull into the closed garage of the safe house, the person will be taken out of the car, and the interrogation will begin. And often, after an interrogation, the person will still be alive. Depending on what they owe and on what they have, they may remain alive for fifteen minutes, or they may be kept for six months or any amount of time in between. Imagine: six months kidnapped, held in a closet, and given one meal per day.

During all this time, we are working with the family of the kidnapped person, forcing them, extorting them, to hand over all of his property—cattle, ranches, other real estate, jewelry, yachts—whatever they have. Everything that they have. When we plan the kidnapping of a person who owes money, we already have an exact list of his property and what we are going to take away from him. And we send the family a video, after a month or two months or three months, to let them know that their loved one is alive, so they will have confidence that he will be returned to them.

But once everything has been taken away from him and his family, he will be killed right there. It is what they call a *carne asada*, a barbecue. There are people who work in the department called "refrigeration" or "cold meats." These are people in charge of killing, cutting up, and burying the body. People are not always buried in the same place where they are killed. This is very difficult. What happens is that the people are executed, and then they are taken in vehicles to the places that in recent years have been called *narco-fosas*, or narco-graves. I think that here in the border region, that . . . well, let's say that if there are one hundred of these narco-fosas, maybe only five or six of these places have been discovered.

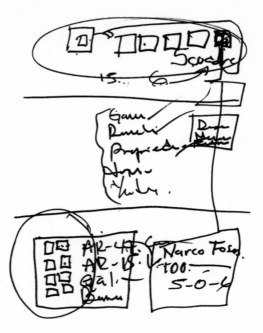

Many stolen vehicles are kept at the safe houses. If the garage will hold ten cars, then that's how many will be kept there. These cars are used to transport executed people and to transport drugs. All of these cars are stolen. When we do a job, these cars will often get wrecked and have to be disposed of.

All of the people working within these organizations have received training in the use of tactical security equipment in the academy—military boots and uniforms, military berets, masks, gloves. They have all been trained to use AK-47s, the guns known as *cuerno de chivo*, or goat's horns, and also AR-15 rifles. The crews also use Gals [an Israeli weapon], Barretts [powerful weapons designed to penetrate armored vehicles], and other rifles that are only issued to the military.

One brings all of this training from the academy. The narcos have already bought and paid for many other people just like me to get this training from the time we enter the police academy. The narcos are simply harvesting the crops that they have planted. And just like me, once the person is determined to no longer be useful to the organization, he will be killed.

• • •

The time comes when these teams are so well trained . . . here, let me explain it a little better. A team or a cell is composed of fifty elements. Of these fifty elements, twenty of them are assigned to guard and transport the drugs. Twenty are dedicated to kidnapping and executing people. And ten are assigned to provide personal security for the person who is in command of the cell.

How many cells are working in the city? In recent years, there have been around . . . well, let's say, for instance, you are talking about the really big guys. . . . For example, "El Chapo"* might have five cells working in Ciudad Juárez in this manner. Don Vicente,** since he is the head of the *plaza*, he might have twenty cells working here. And other groups, not members of either of

---

* Leader of the Sinaloa cartel, Joaquin "El Chapo" Guzman Loera is reputed to be one of the richest men not only in Mexico but in the world. He is said to be currently battling Vicente Carrillo Fuentes for control of the Juárez plaza. See M. J. Stephey, "Joaquin Guzman Loera: Billionaire Drug Lord," *Time*, March 13, 2009, http://www.time.com/time/world/article/0,8599,1884982,00.html.

** Vicente Carrillo Fuentes is allegedly the leader of a large and violent drug-trafficking organization known as the Vicente Carrillo Fuentes Organization. This group is allegedly responsible for the importation of numerous tons of cocaine and marijuana from Mexico into the United States over the Ciudad Juárez–El Paso border annually. See http://www.fbi.gov/wanted/cei/vicente-carrillo-fuentes/view.

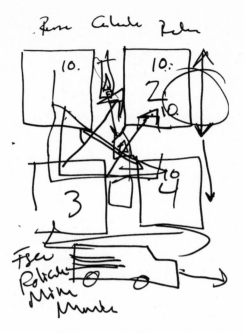

these big cartels, might have a few cells operating here also. Between all of these cells, there is—or there was—an operating agreement. The problem intensified when the personnel of the various cells began to fight among themselves.

One of the most important things that I experienced as a part of this was . . .

He draws a diagram of the cell structure he was part of at that time.

. . . Let's say there were four cells. I was participating in one of these cells, and the cell communicated very well with those here in number four, for example. So that the ten elements of this one and the other one worked hand in hand and could ask for help from each other. But these other ten guys in a different cell were behaving really badly: They were drinking too much, raping women, abusing people, opening up and selling drugs retail, and that was not permitted. So what happened?

It is not as if we had any say-so in this, rather, the orders came from above. They called a meeting together of the cell that was causing trouble. When these people arrived at the meeting they were disarmed, captured, handcuffed, and they were all executed. But it is a really serious problem to transport ten dead men. They will not fit in just any ordinary vehicle. So they used a closed van, escorted by ministerial and municipal police, to take the ten bodies to the place where they would be buried.

But the dead are not always buried.

• • •

I remember a very well known and much talked about case. The order, the direct order, came from a guy who was known as "El Cora." The order was to kill a doctor, Victor Manuel Oropeza. This doctor was also a columnist who wrote for a newspaper in Juárez. The question was: Who was going to do this job? It was going to be difficult to murder someone who was important and who was a renowned journalist in Juárez.

For this reason, none of the cells that were operating at this time in the city wanted to get mixed up in this case. There was, however, a group of five people under the direction of El Cora who dedicated themselves exclusively to executing people in the street. This group took on the order. They made a plan, carried it out, and executed the doctor in his office.

But as is well known, and it has been publicized many times, things did not turn out well. They should have made the murder look like it was the result of a robbery. But because they were not very well prepared, they forgot to take his wallet. They took some money, but then they dropped it and left it there at the scene.

This case was very important. It was a turning point, a key moment, when El Cora came from Sinaloa to Chihuahua to execute people. After this incident that drew so much bad publicity, El Cora and his group began to be stripped of their power. And these were persons of confidence. The murder of the doctor ultimately opened the way for "El Señor de los Cielos," "The Lord of the Skies" [Amado Carrillo, who became the head of the Juárez cartel], to take control of the Juárez plaza.

A little more about El Cora—this was the nickname of a person, "El Cora de Sinaloa." Before the time of El Señor de los Cielos, El Cora commanded a group, together with an army lieutenant, that executed people for the cartel. He moved around all over Sinaloa, Durango, Torreón [a city in the state of Coahuila], Chihuahua, and Sonora. As I understand it, he worked well in all of those states. He was not military, but he had ranking military officers working with him. It was a specialized and professional group that conducted executions. They would arrive at a plaza, carry out their orders to execute someone, and leave. This was their exclusive job—they were specialists. It was not their habit to leave bodies in the street or kill families or carry out gun battles in the streets. At that time [in the late 1980s and early 1990s], El Cora was a person of intelligence. He was aware of the situation. He did not touch women or children. If he was ordered to kill someone, he would do the job and the person would never be heard from again, he would be disappeared, buried.

But at the time of the botched-up murder of Dr. Oropeza, all of the power that El Cora had was being taken away. He could no longer control things here on the border. As different cells began to accumulate more power, each cell began to take on the job of passing drugs into the United States separately. After this, the different groups started looking for easier ways to get drugs into the United States, and this caused new problems. A lot of drug shipments began to be lost. And so a rivalry developed among these five different groups, and they began to fight over the control of the plaza.

In another interview not recorded on tape, the sicario revealed more about this incident. It was important to him because it happened near the beginning of his career in the state police, and El Cora's men had provided some of his training. Because of the prominence of the victim and the publicity at the time, the government mounted an investigation into the murder that led nowhere. In his last columns, Dr. Oropeza had traced the involvement of some police officials with the drug-trafficking organization in the city. The same police officials responsible for investigating the murder were the most likely suspects in the crime. This was covered in both the Mexican and international press at the time, but the sicario knows the details—because he had been called upon to help shelter a comrade in the state police who was one of those involved in the murder.

That's when the team—let's call it the tactical team—that I belonged to began to act. Why do I call it a tactical team? Because it was a team that had knowledge of weapons. We had the skill and dexterity to move all over the city. We knew how to act like police, because we were the police. We knew the schedules of each and every one of the targets because we were constantly investigating them. We had safe houses with machines to gather and record cell-phone calls, including the text messages sent via cell phones—these were all captured and registered.

Every cell had a predetermined number. This one began 229, another 221, 223, 224. . . . And we did not buy the cell phones that we used, they were given to us by the bosses. One was for communicating with family. One was for work. Another was for when the boss needed to talk to us. At my level, at this time, I would have up to eight cell phones. I needed to have direct communication with public security—municipal police, state judicial police, federal judicial police, ministerial police who came from other states, and the special police.

When this problem started,* when they sent the tactical group in to control what was getting out of control, they put together a team that included a sergeant from public security and about forty people. We added another fifty people. It was now a team of ninety men, trained by the military. They knew how to use weapons, defense techniques, how to drive vehicles in chases, how to capture phone calls. They knew systems of interrogation, and they had safe houses all over the city. It was a team of ninety trained men, with the objective of destroying five or six people.** They proved very difficult to get rid of.

This team stayed together for some time, and it was responsible for taking out several high-level commanders of public security. We removed commanders of the state judicial police. At

---

*   The sicario is referring to the chaos unleashed by the murder of Oropeza and the subsequent struggles for control of the Juárez plaza.
**   These people were police commanders in different units.

that time, this team was very very good. I remember once they sent a commander from the federal preventive police to Juárez. He drove an armored Jeep Cherokee. The problem was that this person did not want to come to an agreement with the narco-trafficking organizations. And so, to make him understand how strong this team was, to convince him that his armored Jeep would not function as his security bubble, this vehicle was stolen from outside of the official installations, taken to a park, and burned. Up until this time, this commander had not thought of himself as vulnerable. He thought he was untouchable. But now he understood that there was a really strong organization, that it was very well established, that it had effective strategies, and that its members were corrupt. Therefore, he would need to agree to what he was being asked to do.

After all of this time, after we had managed to arrange things with these first elements of the federal preventive police who had arrived in the state of Chihuahua, what happened next? The narco-trafficking organizations began to control the plaza again, reestablishing some order from the disorder that had occurred. But because now these people—these ninety elements that had been put together—were controlling alcohol, drugs, and other products that were consumed, this group began to be cleaned up. First they formed a group of thirty, and then a group of only fifteen. Of the original ninety, we were reduced to thirty and then to fifteen. What happened to all of the others? I never knew.*

---

* The sicario does not explain or name the groups that were fighting for control of the plaza at this particular time. We believe that these were struggles internal to the Juárez cartel. The point he is making is that the orders to kill would sometimes be carried out against people you had been working with in the recent past and that people at his level carried out orders without asking questions.

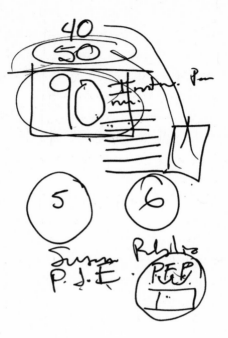

It was very easy for me at this time to be working in Juárez, Chihuahua, Sinaloa, or Durango. All we had to do was arrive at an airport, get on a plane, and go. It was not a problem. Arms and cash were also transported by private planes. In the airport, everything was arranged such that the private flights—small Cessnas—were taken care of in all of the airports by elements of the army. The commercial flights were taken care of by the federal preventive police, and everything was arranged for us. What could not be brought onto the commercial flight due to metal detectors—weapons, or some small amount of drugs, or more than $10,000 or $100,000 cash—was put into a briefcase and delivered to us once we were on the plane.

So, where is this going? This group of fifteen had to travel to Sinaloa, Sonora, Durango, and Chihuahua, where a pact was in force not to touch certain people. This was a pact that had been made with the governor. But we would travel to these states to find people who owed money, and our job was to execute them. When our group was sent, it was not to see if the job would or could be done. Once this group was sent to do a job, it would be completed or else. We knew what we had to do. One of the obligations of this group was that if one of its members was killed or injured, he could not be left behind. In this elite group, the fifteen of us who remained, if one of us fell while carrying out a job, he would have to be recovered and brought out. No one could be left behind.

Unfortunately, I realized . . . it was probably due to the drugs I was taking, from the way I was living . . . I had the feeling that I was untouchable. If anyone looked at me the wrong way, I would confront them: "Hey, what do you want?" And I would just take out my pistol and shoot. . . . But I never had total confidence that if one day I were injured, I never knew for sure that one of my team would take me out with them. I figured it was more likely that they would just take me away and kill me, so as not to leave any loose ends. Looking back now at what has happened to this team of fifteen, I think eight are still alive. Of these eight, I think there are five now working in a team. Of the other three, I don't know. I do not know what happened to them.

• • •

How did I get to the point where I no longer felt any scruples for the people that I killed? I had come to a point in my career and in my life when I was getting paid so much money. This moment comes when they tell you, "We are going to give you $5,000 per month as a salary." But there are some people who are very heavy, very important, and they have a lot of security around them. So then the boss comes back and says, "Let's make a deal. Get rid of this person and we will pay you $45,000. Get your team together and take care of it."

Good.

At some point, when you have all the training, the skills, and the experience, you can do these jobs with no more than four people. But when you are working with a team of only four, none of them can have any fear. If even one of the team is afraid, then the job will fail. When someone is afraid, nerves fail, and the job cannot be carried out. On more than two occasions, we had to cancel a job because of one person who lost his nerve and could not be counted on.

What did we do to be sure, to prepare for the job? First of all, we hardly slept and we took a lot of drugs. We would go for several whole days drinking and taking drugs. Suddenly we get a call. "The person that you are looking for is eating in a certain restaurant." Okay.

So we go, the four of us in two cars, with a third car following in case something goes wrong. One person gets out, another guards the door, and the others look out for the police and for the getaway. What do we want to do with the guy now? This determines what our options are. The first option: confront him and execute him.

He bangs five times on the table,
as if to make the sound of gunshots.

That is one option. Another possibility is that we will have to interrogate him, in which case we need to take him alive. And if we were ordered to take him alive, we would have to take him alive. And there was yet another option: grab him, beat him up, torture him, but not kill him.

The most difficult thing to understand—and one of the most difficult orders to carry out—is that sometimes, when you are in a safe house with a person who is really beaten up and the grave is already dug, then you get the call not to kill him. "Don't let him die."

I remember that on some occasions it happened that they sent us to kidnap someone. Not to execute him, but just to pick him up and to kill him later. So what did we do? We picked the guy up, brought him to a secure location, and then began the work of executing him. When all of a sudden the phone rings. "Wait, wait, it's the boss. . . ."

"Yes, sir. What are your orders, sir? Yes, sir, yes, sir, yes, sir. . . . Yes, yes, yes, sir."

"Stop! Stop!"

The order on this occasion was to revive the person when he was already at the point of death, right on the edge, just seconds away from asphyxiation. We had to revive him, shake him.

"Revive him."

"It's not possible. Sir, we need a doctor, we cannot get him up, the work was very advanced, sir. Yes, sir."

For the narcos, there are no limits.

In just a few minutes a doctor arrived—not an ambulance, of course, but a qualified doctor. The doctor revived the person and left him there with us in stable condition. And we took charge again.

Five, ten, fifteen, even thirty days can go by, and it is no problem, because our job was just to keep the person alive. That is what we were there for—to watch over and guard him, to keep him alive until we received another call.

When this happens, it is a liberation, for us as well as for him.

"Yes, sir, what are your orders? We are here, sir, waiting. No, no, he is fine. He's eating. What is he eating? *Ha!* No, no, he is okay . . . gaining strength. Ah, ah. Okay, sir, as you wish."

This time, our friend was not so lucky. It could be that his family had already paid. It could be that to keep him alive was just to be safe, for insurance, or perhaps he was needed alive for a time, to talk to the family. . . . But the work and the order that followed after the call was: Do away with him. Finish him off.

Now, after he had already been saved once at the point of being strangled to death, this time there was no turning back. This time there was no second call. This time we had to pull the string, and pull it hard.

The sicario begins to describe the ways of torturing people to get information, and he draws in the notebook as he speaks.

Now, there are various ways of killing these people. And none of them are very agreeable. The easiest is just to shoot them. But almost none of the bosses wants them to die quickly or easily. So what do you do? Suffocate them, make them suffer, take out their fingernails one by one, put needles under their fingernails. There are techniques to make them talk.

Here is the body, for example. You soak the clothes with water and then connect ten-caliber cables from the body to the electrical outlet so that it will withstand the voltage from the electricity . . . these cables are attached to their big toes. And you connect this to the electrical power. After two applications of this for ten seconds each, the person will tell you whatever you want, whatever you want. There were some who were very strong who could withstand this. So, for them, there is another technique.

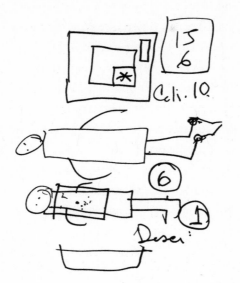

The person is lying down completely naked. We cover the body with a sheet, sprinkle gasoline or alcohol onto the sheet, and when it is soaked, light it with a match. As the fuel burns, it removes up to three layers of skin from their bodies. Their backs would be left completely raw. We might use a liter of alcohol on them. The suffering is enormous.

And there are other forms of interrogation, things that you cannot imagine.

• • •

Sometimes there were people who we would have to care for as long as six months. There were mistakes, and we would get orders to heal these people before we could let them go back to their families. Six or eight months might have passed, and their families had had no knowledge of them. They might be allowed to live, but they could never, never, never see the faces of any of those in the group that had kidnapped them. If they even once saw even one of our faces, they would immediately be killed. No one in this life after such suffering would be able to forget the faces of those who caused it and not try to get revenge. And these are not people without money or power. These are usually people with money, and they would have the means to seek revenge.

Now, a couple of things about following orders. In military school there is a saying: That there are always just two soups, noodle soup or "fuck-you" soup, *sopa de fideo o sopa de jodeo*. And they've always just run out of noodle soup. There is nothing left but the fuck-you soup. And that is what you get.

And the other: Orders are to be obeyed, not discussed. An order would never be discussed. We were there to solve problems for the people we worked for. They trained us to act. They did not ask us our opinions about what to do or not to do with a person. They just gave us orders, and our job was to carry them out. Not one of us—man or woman—would ever be allowed to give our opinions and we could never yield, we could never give in.

• • •

I can tell you that several years ago we brought a guy to this very room. A group of three of us was sent to kidnap an individual who owed money. He had been gambling on horse races and dog races, and he was spending money that was not his. And once it was found out that he had not paid and was losing money, they sent our group to get him.

We were friendly, went to his house, knocked on the door, and picked him up. He came out voluntarily, and we told him he had to come with us. We needed to talk to him. And by chance or destiny, we ended up in this very room with him.* Everything was fine when we got here. We sat down to talk a little. When he realized what was going on, that our mission, our assignment, was to get the money from him, he tried to force his way out. So it was necessary to hit him a few times, tie him up, put on hand-cuffs, gag him so that he could not scream, and he had to stay locked up in the bathroom, in the bathtub, for a few hours.

And we relaxed, watched TV, we ordered some hamburgers and pizza. After a time, I talked to him in the bathroom.

"Here is the situation. You don't have a problem. The problem is the money that you owe. If you pay the money—we know you have the money, some properties, so pay up—then you can go free."

He gave me a sign that he was okay, that he understood. So I said to him, "Look, if you behave, I'll take the gag off. I need for you to talk to your family, tell them to get the money together and pay the money that you spent that did not belong to you and deliver all of the money that you can."

When he made a sign that he understood, I went back out and relaxed a little watching TV. One of the group left. For a while I was with the guy alone. I let him out of the bathroom and let him sit on the bed. I moved the handcuffs from behind his back to in front. I sat him down on the bed, and we were talking a little.

---

* Room 164, the same motel room the sicario had chosen as the place to tell his story.

"You feel relaxed now?"

"Yes."

"Are you ready to talk to your family and tell them to deliver the money that you spent that wasn't yours?"

"Yes."

Then the first time when I gave him the phone . . . I sensed that he was getting ready to say something bad. To tell them that he was kidnapped. So I grabbed the phone and hit him and did not let him talk again for a half hour or more. I called another one of the guys and told him that he needed a little therapy— physical therapy.

So we took him into the bathroom and gave him some physical therapy in the bathtub, forcing his head under one, two, three times in the bathtub full of water. He was gasping for breath.

I said, "So, are you okay now? You know we are not kidding, right? Do the right thing and you will be fine."

He did not want to talk to the other guys, so they left and he talked to me. "What do you want me to do?"

"Nothing, just talk to your family and ask them to get the money that you spent that did not belong to you and deliver the money. Correct?"

In this moment I could tell he had some confidence in me because I had not treated him as badly as the other guys. And aside from this, we are trained to control these kinds of situations. I took off the handcuffs and gave him the phone.

"Here, call. Tell them to get the money together and tell them that they will get another call telling them where they need to deliver it."

That evening, about six or seven, he made the other call, very calm, and then I let him sleep in the bed for an hour or so. Later that night we put the handcuffs back on and put him back in the bathtub. We had to threaten him a little.

The next day he was okay, pretty calm. He liked Italian food, so we let him order some to be delivered. He had more confidence in us. The next day they delivered half of the money that he owed. Another day went by to give them time to deliver more of the money. By that time, he was calm and walking around the room, watching TV, resting on the bed. His hands were cuffed, but in front. He trusted me, and he said, "Look, I'm sorry for what I did. I was wrong to spend the money. I was drinking a lot and losing at the races. . . . But everything is going to come out okay, right, as long as they keep paying?"

I told him, if it wasn't okay, he would not be walking around. "You would not even be here like this. You would not even be here."

And he said to me, "I promise, I'll never remember you, what you look like."

And I told him not to worry, that he was paying and it was okay. On the third day, in the morning they delivered another part of the money. And before ten thirty that morning—he was lying down on the bed—we got a call that we needed to deliver him to the other side of the border. And so that is what we did. He went out without handcuffs, got in the backseat of the car. He asked where we were taking him. I said everything was okay, the boss just wants to talk to you. There's no problem, you paid, but you have to go and see the boss.

He left in confidence, and I never knew anything more about him. We never heard anything about him again. Here in this room, I realized that he had confidence in me, he opened up and confessed all of his errors and pleaded with me. "You are right, I was wrong, spending this money that was not mine. I should not have done what I did, but nothing like this will happen again. It was the first time I ever did anything like that in all the years I've worked for this person."

He made one mistake, and it would cost him his life.

But in this moment, even though we knew he had paid, we could not commit the error of saying, "Okay, you paid, now go free." We had nothing to do with making those kinds of decisions. *No somos ni juez, ni parte.* We are not judge, nor party in this case.

• • •

For some time, six to eight months or more, I was working inside the police, kidnapping people and then handing them over to other people. The advantage of being a policeman while also working for the narco-trafficking organizations is that you can play both sides. Supposedly, you are working to protect people and society, but at the same time, you are getting paid a lot of money to do jobs required by the narco-traffickers, to deliver people to them.

During this time, they gave us a lot of drugs and alcohol for free. It was difficult to get drugs in Juárez. We had to cross over to El Paso to get drugs because at this time it was not allowed to open up packages and use drugs that were passing through Juárez. This arrangement lasted for some time. We would get calls. We were always drinking. In the official police squad car, we would always carry a cooler in the trunk with beer, liquor, soda, and mineral water for mixing drinks, stuff to eat. We never did any work investigating robberies or anything like that. Since we were chosen by the heads of the cartel, they paid off the municipal police not to bother us. We always had to be available if the narcos needed us for a job. We could not be busy doing regular police work on the street. There were maybe seven hundred or nine hundred police agents who were not mixed up directly with the narcos, and they had to do all of the regular police work required for the society.

I remember one time when we got a call . . . at that time there were not many cell phones. They were really big things, we called them "bricks," the really early kinds of cell phones. I can tell you that I tried out some of the first ones that were used in Juárez that had American numbers. So we get a call on the cell phone that there is this guy at a mall and that we have to go and pick him up and turn him over. So why do we get the call?

Well, back at that time, they would put people to the test. There was a certain time period (a kind of probation) at the beginning of your career with them. It's not like the military or the police career, but ninety days, and of those, maybe thirty days shut up in a house, another thirty days of some other kind of training, and another thirty days to learn the techniques of kidnapping people. This time they called us, and so we go out to the mall.

He draws a diagram of the operation.

Here is the parking lot where we waited for the people to come out. They give us the description of the people we are looking for. Okay. So we get into our squad car. I can tell you that I was always really high. If this happened on a Friday, we would have been drinking, doing drugs, and partying since Monday. And we would hardly have slept one day in all of that time. For us, working was a party. We would do drugs and go to a hotel

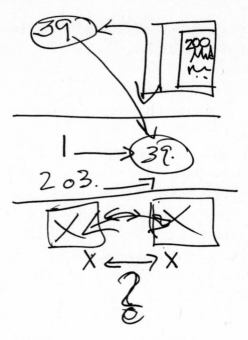

with some girls and go out with them. They didn't call on us to do many jobs at that time.

But this time when they called us, things took a different turn. In the police, there are codes, numbers, and letters. . . . You could say X-2, X-Z, Z-2, X-1. . . . These are codes we use so we don't have to talk so much on the radio. So after we picked up these people and were driving around with them, this giant cell phone—the "brick"—rings, and the only thing we hear is an order using a number that they were using at this time.

He writes the number 39 in the notebook.

And hearing this number—this code—we knew this was an order that meant that the person needed to die immediately. I never doubted at the moment I got the order, I never doubted,

I just pulled the trigger. I could not even think. I did not know the person, it was not a family member. For me, it was nobody. I simply obeyed an order. We received a call, we picked up a person, we carried him around for a while, we got the call with the order, and we carried out the order . . . immediately.

I did not fully realize what I had done until two or three days later when I was finally sober. I realized how easy it was that the drugs and the world that I was in were controlling and manipulating me. I was no longer myself. I was no longer the young person who had had a strong desire to serve my society. I was no longer the man who wanted to get married and have a family. I was a person who was nothing but the things that I was commanded to do.

I followed orders.

I realized at this moment that I never doubted that I would carry out any order that I was given. Even though it was for such a terrible career as this that I had to put my life on the line.

He draws a rectangle bisected by a diagonal line and the words "AUTHORITY/NARCO."

On several occasions, there were confrontations. Thank goodness we came out okay. Not because there were a lot of us, but because we knew how to do our job very well. We knew the techniques, we knew the weak points of the person that we were going to kidnap or execute. As I told you before, we always studied our adversaries. Nothing was done quickly or casually. We did not just see the target and make the hit. You have to see and study ahead of time how to do it, how to handle the moment when you confront the target. You have to know what you will do when you come face to face with your adversary.

Times have changed. Nowadays, the technique is to kill on sight, at the moment of confrontation: "Wherever I find you, I kill you." But this is because there are no more real codes, no more rules in the business. Before, the different cartels that were working in the country respected the codes and arrangements that had been established. Now, there are no codes, they are all lost. Now it is just: You owe me, you pay me.

• • •

I remember really well when the Mexicles and the Aztecas—two enemy gangs—were fighting for power in the CERESO [*Centro de Readaptación Social (Center for Social Rehabilitation)*, the state prison]. Then there was a problem, and they contacted us.

"Look, we have a problem because they can't come to an agreement, and it is affecting the sale of drugs inside and outside the country."

So it was necessary to kidnap the leaders of the Aztecas and the Mexicles on the outside. This was during the time that I was active. And they were forced to meet, and they were questioned about their problems and about why their people were not be-

having and working as they should. Finally they came to an agreement to achieve equality and peace inside of the CERESO prison.

A lot of the work—the majority of it—that the cartel man-
ages is done from inside of the prisons. Many of the executions
are ordered from inside of the prisons. Why? Because the prisons
in Mexico have become manufacturing centers and packing houses
for drugs to be shipped to many places in the United States.

• • •

*He reflects back again on the test he was given at the beginning of
his career, when he did his first killing at the age of just eighteen.*

Back then, that time we picked up the guy and killed him in
the car . . . what can I say? This was a trial by fire, this order to
pick up this guy and kill him. And it was so simple to carry out
that order and just kill the guy. So he's dead, now what do we
do? Get rid of the body. Throw him out. We are driving around
in an official police squad car, wondering: How can we just toss
out a dead body? So we call and ask. "Where do you want us to
dump the body?"

And the answer came: "That is your problem, not mine.
What do you think we pay you for?"

So then you realize that you need to start looking for places
to dump a dead body. . . . It really isn't that hard. I was feeling
so bad, all drugged up and drunk, that the only thing we could
figure to do—I remember it really clearly—was to toss him in the
sewer, so we passed over an open manhole and dumped him in.

From that moment, my life changed in relation to the position that I had in the organization. When you cease to have any
doubt and do not hesitate to carry out an order and you just get

it done, a real clean job, people start to notice and you realize that their eyes are on you. "Hey, you see what he did?" After two or three days, you start to hear them talking. "You know what? He did it and he didn't feel anything."

Well, shit, how could you feel anything with all the drugs you are taking? But when you sober up there is nothing left for you except to keep doing the jobs. You cannot look back. Anything else and you'll end up like the dead guy. And that is what I did. It is what formed my hard character. This is when I began to realize that the man who had dreamed of having a family, the boy who had been my mother's pride and joy. . . . She always said, "He gets really good grades, he is going to be somebody, he can be anything he wants, a doctor, an engineer, or an architect, because he is ambitious. . . ."

This is when I realized that I was completely bad in my character, in my person, because I was never going to be able to become anything more than I had already become. What this meant was that I was a person who had become *un monigote*, a puppet manipulated by the strings of those who gave me the orders. I no longer had my own life. Your life does not belong to you anymore once you reach this stage in the organization. You depend completely on the person who gives you orders.

For many years, the work went on, and I worked twenty-four hours per day, three hundred sixty-five days per year. I was never able to turn off my radio or my cell phone. The day that it was turned off, it meant you were dead or that they wanted you dead. If you did not have a really good excuse to not answer your radio or telephone, it was because you no longer wanted to know anything, and if it got to that point, well, you could not go on living much longer under those circumstances.

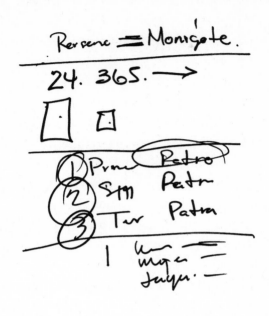

• • •

My intention was to serve. For a long time, I would say: For me, Number 1 was the boss, "El Patron." Number 2 was El Patron. And Number 3 was El Patron. I lived to serve and to defend a person—El Patron. I did whatever the boss told me to do. Any little thing he desired, I would provide it. I could never say, "No, you cannot have it," or, "No, there is none." Anything he wanted, he would have. Anything he wanted to possess, he would possess—cars, women, jewelry. There was never any problem with money for buying cars or jewelry.

But there are many women who are not for sale. Yet, when the boss wanted a woman, it was your job to try to persuade them. Many times . . . an infinity of times . . . I never had any remorse about the things I told them to try to convince them: "A certain person wants to get to know you and go out with you. If you agree to come with us, you will stay for a week in the best hotel on the best beach, and you will have a very pleasant week. If you want money, fine. But you will do whatever is asked of you and afterward are going to forget about the person for the rest of your life. And if you agree, everything will be fine."

Many, many women fell for this and went along with it, and they are alive. But many others believed that they could outsmart us, and I never saw them again. I'm not saying that we murdered all of these women. Even though there were a lot of women, including very young women, who were killed. No, what happened was, there were a lot of very ambitious women, and they wanted to become wives of the bosses at the moment. But the boss already had something like forty "wives." He had women living in every state of Mexico. He certainly didn't need any more wives.

Let's go back and consider the case of Don Amado [Carrillo] and his forty or forty-two wives. He got married whenever he wanted. I mean, they are lovers, not really wives. They would get married, but with false judges. These people (the narco-bosses) would not marry easy women or prostitutes. There are a lot of women that they use just to have fun, and they pay them. But they would look for beautiful women, and in this city . . . they would especially look for those from families with real money. This is one way that rich businessmen get mixed up in narco-trafficking. The daughters of the big *empresarios*—businessmen, entrepreneurs—in Mexico marry narco-bosses as a way to double their fortunes. But without realizing it, they have committed an error. The narcos are using the businesses of their wives to launder

their money. But look at what happens? There are many businesses that are failing. And they will continue to fail.

The women marry them, but they are false marriages. They
will say, "Look, take me to a judge and marry me." The narcos
have the power to have a fake judge appointed, or they can simply buy a marriage certificate from a real judge. If the woman
wants a marriage certificate, they will give it to her, just like they
can provide fake driver's licenses or other kinds of identification
documents like voting credentials or military cards. They are all
false and for sale. It is a game they play, these illusions that they
live under.

If the narcos want something, they will get it, one way or another. Why? Because if they don't get it for the good they will get
it for the bad. And as far as the women are concerned, there is a
saying: "If I want you, I will have you, for better or worse. If I
can't have you one way, I'll have you another way. And if I can't
have you, no one will have you, that will be the end of you, and
there you will be buried. Simple."

So let me repeat what I told you before. There are two soups.
Noodle soup or fuck-you soup. And the noodle soup is all gone.
So you get used to it, make yourself comfortable, or you get
fucked over. That's the truth.

And so, for these women, there is no way out. You get to
know a narco, and he wants you, you will get used to it and
enjoy the life because you have no choice. Jewelry, houses,
bodyguards. . . . "No one else dare look at you because you belong to me. You are my 'queen.' Marry me this minute because I
want you and I will have you."

And then he sets you up in a house, and there you stay for
two or three years. And you cannot leave. It is a golden prison.

This is the truth. These women live in a golden prison. With bodyguards. And they cannot leave until the boss comes and until they are given permission to see him. He may come to town and not even come to the house because in the same city he has four or five other "wives," and he runs out of time, because he has to see all these other adventurous women and have his pleasure with all of them.

• • •

When there were problems with people, the bosses had us to fix things, to keep people under control. There came a moment when there were just five of us that were trusted, and we operated as if we were a team of ten or twenty. At that time, these five people were enough to control the whole plaza. In the sense that we were very well trained and we always had eyes and ears wherever they were needed. They were paid to give us any information that we wanted. And they were not just paid with money. If we needed information at that time, we would get it. And when these were orders from the boss, he would get the information. Many people at this time tried to leave the organization, many people began to have regrets and wanted to get out of the business.

Back then, agents like us who worked for police corporations were receiving a certain quantity of money to get rid of a person—$2,000 or $3,000, it depended on the person's rank. After that, we started to get a lot more money depending on how hard it was to kill the target or how important he was. We described it using the old saying: *Dependiendo del sapo la pedrada*, The stone you throw depends upon the size of the toad. We started getting up to $25,000 for the execution of a person. This is apart from and in addition to our salaries. In order to be able to work freely, it was not enough to just say, "Yes, I'll do the job." These jobs were not assigned casually.

He sketches the organization chart of the corporation.

It begins with the head of the corporation, below him are the group bosses, and below them, the agents. And at all levels, those who are involved receive monthly salaries, a certain quota every month. And for people who had been recruited, like me, since before I was even in the police academy, and who received a salary to attend the academy, it was not difficult. Those of us who had been involved since that time were the most trusted. When there was an operation, even some of the group bosses were under our orders. As agents, we would sometimes give the orders to some of the bosses. It shouldn't have been that way, but at the time, those were the orders coming from above. The bosses could not be given all of the information. Sometimes the only thing they did was act as a smokescreen for us to do our job.

• • •

There were times when many people made mistakes and tried to traffic independently, passing trailers full of drugs at the army roadblock south of Juárez that was called "Precos" at that time, but I'm not sure what it is called now. They would try to pass a trailer by saying, "This merchandise belongs to the cartel and it is protected." But the soldiers that were there would just ask a few questions and then let it pass.

Coming into the city of Juárez there was a *glorieta*, a traffic circle. I'm not sure if it is still there. Just past this intersection was a place to review the plates and details of the trucks and trailers passing. People working for us would separate out the loads.

Okay. "You say that this trailer belongs to the cartel. Who do you work for?"

"I work for so-and-so." This one or the other.

So the load would be taken to a warehouse for security along with the trailer, the driver, and usually a truck with three or four guys behind and a car with two other guys. But when this happened—when people thought they could outsmart the cartel by passing these drugs—the cartel that did not own these drugs would just confiscate them. They would take all of the cargo and kidnap all of the guys carrying it—maybe six or seven people altogether—who would then end up buried in seven more graves in one of the many clandestine cemeteries in this city.

I cannot tell you exactly how many people have been buried in this fashion. It is impossible to say. Personally, I cannot say exactly, for instance, that I was present at one hundred executions and that these people are buried in a certain place. No, no, it is not possible to say for sure. There could have been thousands more such executions. The cartel has a lot of safe houses and many people under their command. There are places that have been discovered where thirty, thirty-six, forty, and in another place ten or more bodies are buried—these are all in safe houses.

But this is nothing compared to those safe houses that are properties belonging to rich people that have been rented by the cartel. The people owning these houses have no idea that there might be up to thirty, forty, or fifty people buried on these properties. The graves are not small, they are deep and very large. The odor of the decomposing bodies is very fetid. It is necessary to put lime and other chemicals on the bodies, remove all of their clothing and other belongings so that the bodies will not leave any traces, so that they cannot be located or identified.

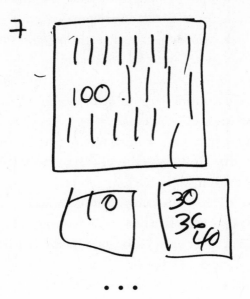

. . .

As long as the victims were men, killing them was no problem for me. In most cases, they were executed because they were stealing or they owed money and were not paying. When this happens and it is a man, there was no problem. The problem that I had—and it was a serious problem that began to convince me that I had to change my life—was when they began to kidnap women. When women began to work for the cartel, and I started to realize what was going on. . . .

In reality, not I, nor my close friends, nor my wife, realized many things.* But the heads of the cartel have eyes and ears

---

* The sicario mentions the woman he was married to at this time, early in his career. Later in his story, they become separated. He currently lives with his second wife.

everywhere. And they would know when a woman was going around with someone or talking too much. And they would just give us the address in this street in this neighborhood, this is her car, license tags, here is her description. . . . "Okay, go pick her up."

You would wait for her outside of her house, put her in the car, and take her to a safe house.

It is very ugly to see a woman tortured. It is very ugly to see the outrages that are done to them because the people doing this have no scruples. It is not the same thing as dealing with a man who knows he has been stealing, who owes money, and who has tried to disappear without paying what he owes. It is not the same to see a woman suffer until she begs for mercy, to see her violated, raped not by one but by five or six or seven men . . . and then to make her suffer until she loses consciousness.

He draws the line.

And finally. . . . Oh, it is terrible to strangle them, at times like this it is better to just shoot them. To strangle a person, it is so horrible, to feel how they suffer, to see how they lose all hope. It is to feel how their life slips away from them little by little. It is to see that the person has a line and the moment comes when they are on the line, when they are dying, and all of the strength they are exerting to get free starts to dissipate and their body is ceasing to function, their life is slipping away. But no, then you can loosen the hold on them a little, and they gain a little strength and start to revive a little. It is necessary to make it last a long time so that the asphyxiation is slow and induces much suffering.

• • •

After this, you start to learn the ways that the cartels leave messages according to how they leave the bodies of the people they have killed. The orders are like this. Throw the body face up. This is a message. Throw the body face down. This is another message. Cut a finger off and put it in the mouth. Message. Cut a finger off and put it in the anus. Message. Take out the eyes. Cut out the tongue. These are situations that without being a doctor or medic. . . .

Translator's note: I had made a mistake by writing to ask him to explain these messages. He insisted that we meet and he would tell me in person. When we met that day he brought a printout from a website: "Señales del narco y su interpretación" ("Narco-Signs and Their Interpretation"). He told me that this was pura fantasia (pure fantasy) . . . and explained.*

---

* As of November 21, 2010, the website (http://www.regioblogs.com/2008/06/07/senales-del-narco-y-su-interpretacion) was no longer available.

About the messages left by the narcos, the fact is, to kidnap someone and kill them sends a very clear message: That the person is directly damaging the interests of the narcos. For example, when the person is given the *tiro de gracia* [*coup de grâce*], this is to secure the objective. It is not enough just to shoot the person because he could remain alive, and if he survives he could identify those who shot him.

About torture—it is not always for the purpose of getting information. There are people who torture because of spite, anger, because the person owes them something, because the person might have gone out with their girlfriend. . . . That's how the narcos operate—whatever they want they take.

When a person is found *encobijado*, killed and left in the open wrapped in a blanket—it is not necessary that the person is someone important or respected. Even *cholos* [*young street gangsters*] sometimes show up as encobijados—there are a lot of imitators out there. The message is not a real one.

When they cut off a finger and insert it in the mouth or ear or anus . . . it is because they need to send some kind of message, but this doesn't happen very often, and the person who does it had better know how to cut off the parts without making a bloody mess. Now, it is very difficult to know how to kill the person, to wait until the circulation of blood stops, and then to cut off the different parts of the body. . . .

To know what the messages mean, you also have to look at where the bodies are left, where they are thrown. . . . Will they be seen by the people who are intended to see them?

Nowadays, the narcos don't have to work very hard to let people know what they want them to know. If the narcos hang a sign on a bridge, it is like broadcasting it on that TV show *Todo Mexico se entere* [*All Mexico Finds Out*].

The press is so corrupt. They know that if they don't publish these sensational signs, then the news won't sell. They are happy when the narcos put these signs up because it sells newspapers like you can't imagine. And so the narcos don't have to go to very much trouble to get their messages out. The newspapers do the work for them.

A person might have his hands cut off because he was involved in things he should not have been involved in. Or he took things that did not belong to him.

But really, what can people on the outside understand about these things when the messages are intended for those inside the narco business? A lot of people see these things, and so they think they know what is going on. Ah, they cut off his hands! What does it mean? It is something between them, the narcos. People should not even pay attention to these messages. I think the press is doing harm by sensationalizing and publicizing such things.

There are other ways of leaving messages. It doesn't serve the interests of the narcos if, after they have kidnapped and killed someone, the body is found. The fact is, bodies have been dug up in many cities in Mexico, and I can tell you that these bodies should show a certain level of decomposition when they are found. But without a little more investigation and professional work, to find out if the body is face up or face down, or if there is lime or not, or salt or sugar or some other chemical used on the body. . . .

Why? Because to bury the body face down or face up—that sends a real message, and you can give something like that a certain importance. For example, if the body is buried face down, it is because the narcos never wanted that body to come to light. So when the body is found, it means that someone informed.

And if someone informs, they will be found out because the narcos have ways of knowing who it was that provided the information.

You receive your orders and you carry them out. Once you know that the person is asphyxiated and dead, you can cut off any part of the body without a problem, and it will not bleed very much. The blood ceases to circulate. I remember well once when a person made a mistake and began to beat up one of the *enfermos*, the sick ones. We sometimes called our victims our "patients." He kicked the guy in the face and tore his head open and got reprimanded for doing this. "Why are you scolding me? He's going to die anyway," and he kept yelling and beating on the guy.

And so they provided a very logical explanation. "If you kick the guy in the head before he is dead, you'll have to pick up the carpet and clean up everything because it will make such a disgusting bloody mess. First kill the person. Then cut off anything you want."

This is not something you learn in the academy. This is not something you learn in military school. This kind of thing you must learn in life.

• • •

There comes a moment when the smallest thing annoys you so much, not because you are so good, but because your mind is so messed up from drugs and drinking that you do not feel any scruples for what you do. The moment comes, and you might be driving down the street in your car, and you pass another car and "Hey, you? Why are you looking at me like that?" Okay, and so you just take out a gun and shoot without knowing who the person is and for nothing except that the person has looked at you the wrong way. These incidents happened a lot at one time, until a higher-ranking person in the organization prohibited this kind of thing in order to stop so many unjustified killings.

• • •

At one time, an arrangement was made that violent deaths would not be allowed to take place in the city of Chihuahua, the state capital, that this city was protected by an agreement. But killings continued to take place in Parral, Delicias, Camargo, Juárez, Durango, Torreón. So anyone in Chihuahua who was a target would have to be picked up from the city and taken to another place to be killed—from Chihuahua to Torreón or Durango or from Chihuahua to Juárez or to some other city. This is not just a simple transfer—get in the car and let's go. There are certain logistics that we would have to follow using back roads to avoid encountering soldiers and military roadblocks.

When I left my training the first thing that I was told was: There is an arrangement with public security. There is an arrangement with both the state and federal judicial police. There is an arrangement with the federal preventive police. All of these corporations have been "fixed" or corrupted. But there is no arrangement with the army. If you have a problem and the army detains you, you will have to arrange that on your own. We can save you from all of the other agencies, but there is no arrangement with the army. At that time, the army was not corrupted.

With the passing of time, I'm talking about four or five years, a moment came when, during the fiestas that we had on the ranches, we had really great bands playing for our parties. Bands as famous as Los Tigres del Norte, Los Tucanes. . . . And at the very best tables, there were military leaders sitting, right there in the front row. What had never, ever been arranged before, had now been taken care of. Someone, a very powerful person, had come along, and this person had made the arrangements with the army. And it was because of this new arrangement that the narcos began to work with the military.[*]

This new situation brought about many changes to the ideology of the sicario and to the way the work was carried out. Now it was no longer easy to compete with those people who tried to imitate the work. There were those who sold very small quantities of drugs, and they would go around bragging, "I'm a narco, and if you owe me or steal $50 worth of drugs from me, I'm going to kill you." This is ridiculous. No one in the cartel would kill for $50. These were imitators. And what the rise of these imitators meant was that the city started getting more corrupted and out of control. It meant that no one could trust anyone, and that no one was going to be respected. And so an attempt was made to try to clean up this situation—that was when contact was made with the leaders of the prison gangs—and this conversation took place not just in Mexico but also in the United States.

• • •

*In the following passage, the sicario describes
a large operation involving all of the different
police corporations, the military, and the Juárez cartel
operatives working together to regain control over the city.*

---

[*]   He is not certain but estimates this date as sometime in August 2003 because he remembers that it coincided with the birth of one of his children.

One year, the moment arrived and the order came down that in thirty days exactly, *no one*, absolutely *no one*, would be allowed to sell a single packet of cocaine. Not even a tiny amount could be sold in Juárez. No one would be able to do it. Why? There was an announcement that something like three thousand kilos of cocaine had been lost. But the small-time sellers who were causing problems for the cartel that was in control of the plaza did not pay attention to this order because they had never really understood the power of the organization and they thought that they could disobey the orders of the cartel. So what happened? The people who had stolen these drugs and who were selling it on their own were identified and executed. We are talking about a massive execution of about seventy people.

Somewhat earlier, there had been another problem, this time with car thieves. No one was in control over what they were doing. It developed into a real problem, and the police themselves asked for help from the cartel to dismantle these gangs of car thieves. So there was another massive cleanup of a group of some forty-five young punks* who were dealing in stolen cars.

When these people were rounded up, the operation was not carried out by just one group. You could never say that it was done only by sicarios working for the cartel. The operation also included elements of the municipal police and the state and federal judicial police working with the cartel. We are talking about some eight hundred elements working together to get rid of this

---

* The sicario indicated that these young men were not street gangsters, but were from middle-class families and had begun to talk too much about their criminal activities in Juárez bars and discos. They had to be eliminated because they were seen as a threat to the arrangement between the government and the cartel.

group of seventy dealers and the other group of forty-five car thieves who were causing a lot of trouble.

And these bodies are now buried in various colonias and houses throughout the city. And these are bodies that are never going to see the light of day. Or in the case that someday these bodies are found, they will never be identified. If it is difficult to recognize five bodies buried in a common grave, how do you ever think that it will be possible to identify seventy people in a mass grave when they have been put into the ground many years ago completely naked?

Not all of these people died immediately. Among those who were kidnapped, there were a dozen or more of them who were held and given the chance to live for several days before being killed. Why? Because they knew people inside the cartel and they had earned a special privilege. Because they were people who were working in some capacity as informants for the cartel. And others were informants for the police. And not just for the police in Mexico, but some of them had crossed over to the United States to give information to the police agencies there about what was going on in Mexico.

These people received a very special treatment. I remember one time when we heated up two-hundred-liter tubs of water. The people were tied up at the shoulders, their bodies suspended over the tub using a winch, and they were lowered little by little into the boiling water. When they fainted, they were taken out of the water and there was a doctor there who revived them. And then parts of their bodies were cut off—parts that were completely burned, cooked. And they would revive and react once again, and they were lowered again into the water little by little until they finally died. These deaths are not the work of a sicario.

203. ——→.

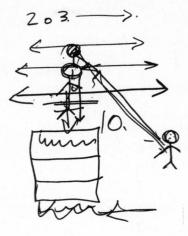

10.

Sicario. Preferencia.

5,000.

1 de Inmediata
Ya Balazo.
Cuchillada.
Golpe . .

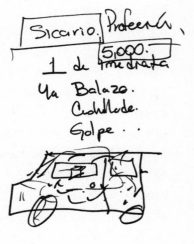

Porque no
dató. Con

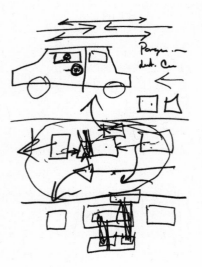

This is the work of sick people. Sick people. People who enjoy seeing the suffering of another.

THE FUNCTION OF A SICARIO

The function of a sicario is to do away with a person immediately. Whether by a bullet or a knife or a blow, so quick and clean that the person feels nothing.

If you are going to kill someone in a car, for example, when a sicario is a professional, he does not do it like any imitation sicario. Here is the car and the target is driving and you have to kill him. An imitator shoots up the whole car . . . *bam bam bam bam bam* . . . spitting bullets all over the place. When a real sicario works and has a target and the target is driving, he makes a tight circle with the bullets right here through the car door where it will hit the target near his heart, or here through the windshield where it will hit the target in the head. This is the work of a sicario. The rest are imitators.

A real sicario has no need to make the person suffer. Because the person is already suffering from the first moment that he knows he is being followed. There is something that he feels, even if the target has nerves of steel, even if he is very strong, he feels it and he suffers.

Among the jobs that have been done, there are various ways of targeting the objective in the car. You might have a car stop in front and one behind—there is always a car behind that helps to avoid crossfire. One car pulls up alongside the target car to shoot. Several other cars will trap the objective in his car so that he cannot escape. Once the target is shot, the various cars leave the scene all going in different directions. There are ways of doing it so that there is no crossfire.

There are difficult moments when the order is to . . . well, there can be some mistakes, and sometimes one of your close companions ends up being the target. This is very difficult because the order comes to do away with one of our own. You can never ask why. The only one who knows why is the person who gives the order, and that is the boss. And the boss never makes a mistake. And if he makes a mistake, it is possible that the order will come again. That is, the order will be given to do away with anyone who might know that the original order might have been in error. These moments were very difficult for me. And if the order comes and you are ordered to kill a person who is your own companion. . . . Many times there are mistakes. . . .

• • •

But during your trajectory through life, there comes a moment when you hit a roadblock, you reach your limit. And so when the day came and I hit my limit, I suddenly stopped drinking, I stopped smoking, and I stopped consuming drugs. I said to myself: "No more." This day was a lot of fun for the person above me, my boss at the time.

He says, "You want some *perico*, some cocaine?"

"No thank you."

"How about a drink?"

"No thanks, sir."

"Cigarette?"

"No thank you, sir."

He was shocked and started laughing at me. "What's happening with you?"

"No more for me."

"Will you be able to handle the work sober?"

"I am the one who does the work, not the cocaine, the alcohol, or the cigarettes."

But I knew that in my life something was causing me to change. And that to always be drugged or drunk did not allow me to think clearly or completely about what I needed to do. When I began to take this step and when they started making fun of me, I started to feel persecuted by my own companions and coworkers. It was difficult to see how when I moved from one hotel to another . . . because I never lived in the safe houses. Just like this motel room, the safe houses were only to be used for a time to do a job, and then they would be abandoned. The only time I stayed in a safe house was if I had to stay to take care of somebody who had been beaten up or to carry out an interrogation.

When I found that I needed to move about from place to place, I knew the techniques for doing that. I had helped many of my companions and coworkers and trained them in how to follow people and keep them under surveillance. So when this happened to me, when I tried to get away, it was less than two days before I realized that I was being followed and followed and followed. And then the day came that I decided to confront the person who was in charge of me.

CHILD
OF GOD

I remember one time when I was leaving one of the safe houses and heading for a hotel. I had figured out earlier that I was being followed by my own companions. But this did not worry me too much. This is very common when someone stops drinking and taking drugs. It usually means one of two things. First, it may mean that the person is going to spend some time at home for a change. The second possibility is that he wants to run away, to get out of the life altogether. So the bosses are on guard regarding these situations. If the bosses say, "Here, have a drink," then you have to drink. If they say, "Smoke," you have to smoke. If they tell you to take drugs, you have to do it.

They know that if a person is not under the influence of any substances, then they are going to be really top-notch because they are fully aware of all of their five senses. At this time, my normal state was to drink about a liter of whiskey every day, a *cuarta* of cocaine (which is quite a few grams because we were snorting it all day long), and smoke one or two packs of cigarettes. This was my normal condition. When people saw me consuming cocaine, it was no problem for me because I didn't care if people were there or not. I might be talking to someone and do drugs at the same time. . . . There are places where you can buy hits [*he says "balas" (bullets)*], and you can get it really fast. You just turn your back and inhale a line of cocaine, you don't have to fool around with papers or anything. And since the death of Amado Carillo, cocaine has become easily available anywhere in Juárez.*

When you stop doing drugs, the person in charge of you starts to worry. I figured it was normal that they started following me and keeping me under surveillance. I seldom went to my house. I would sleep there one or two days and then go twenty or twenty-five days without going home. Why? For security. I always tried to keep them from knowing where I lived. I always had a room in a motel or friends with safe houses where I could go for a few hours and then go someplace else. Or go to a motel and shower, change clothes. Or I would invite some girls to go out and then return to some other place to sleep.

---

* It was Amado Carrillo, head of the Juárez cartel between 1993 and 1997, who forbade the sale of cocaine in Juárez. Since his death, drugs have become more available and no cartel leaders or government officials have been able to completely control the domestic drug market.

But when I stopped drinking, smoking, and using drugs, this was something that my bosses didn't like. I stopped hanging out so much in hotels and started going home a lot more. This situation worried my bosses and my coworkers. What is going on with him? What is he up to? He is not the same person as before.

The only thing about getting off the drugs and alcohol that was beneficial to me was that it made the work I was doing at that time even better. When I quit drinking, smoking, and doing drugs I realized that I no longer functioned at 100 percent. I started to function at 200 percent. My work got so much better. I was stronger, faster, more aggressive. My instincts were sharper than ever. I did not hesitate. . . . When I got an order from a superior, I learned to look at his eyes, his body language, and even if his back was to me, I would see how he moved his head, his shoulders, his hands . . . and I would know what he was going to tell me before he spoke. I learned, and these senses got even sharper. When I quit these vices, instead of the work being harder, I began to be even better than before—better and sharper than ever.

I was so much better that I began to realize that on the way to my house I would always, always encounter this sign. It was a big billboard and it said:

IF YOU HAVE PROBLEMS, CALL UPON HIM.

And a phone number. Well, I saw this sign every day, every single day for one or two months. Every day.

During these months, when they were anticipating a situation with me, I was going to be ready. Once we had to do a job in a discotheque with a bar here.

He sketches this out.

So here is the entrance. When they came in through this entrance, I was there accompanying the person I was guarding. Over here was an exit. I would never leave through the same door that I had entered. I easily got away by leaving through the back way, where an armored vehicle was waiting with people that I trusted at the ready. These were people I had chosen for the job who did not drink or smoke or do drugs.

The moment came when the change in me, in my character, was so radical that they doubted that I was not doing drugs. I had done so much in the past. "What are you doing, what are you taking?" They thought I was on some other kind of drug. I said, "No, nothing. I don't want it anymore." I told them that I was completely fed up, that I just could not do it anymore. I had taken drugs and used alcohol for practically my whole life. I couldn't take it anymore.

• • •

Oh, there were times when I slept.

Here's the bed, the pillow. Here on one side an AK-47, here at the end of the bed an AR-15, underneath a 9mm, or a 38-super. If there was a sound, I was so stressed that if I heard the least little sound, I would wake up immediately ready to shoot. Many times I did not go to my house because I felt so tense, so on edge, that if my wife made some sound or if I heard something that startled me while she was sleeping next to me, I was afraid that I would do something to hurt her. I could not tell the difference between a member of my family or an enemy.

There is a saying: "Never leave an enemy alive." Because he will come looking for you and he will kill you. So for me, it was very difficult to sleep without my weapons. When I was doing a lot of drugs, I barely slept. I would doze off a little. Then I would have to get up, shower, and start doing drugs and drinking again. I would leave the house and sometimes get a motel room. And since I was alone, I would put the Do Not Disturb sign out. And pass a day or a day and a half sleeping. Completely alone. No one else in the room. I would pay for three or four days. Do not disturb. I would close everything and it would be very dark, and I would sleep and sleep and sleep.

When my colleagues began to see these changes in me, the moment came when I managed to escape from those who had me under surveillance. Due to the fact that I had trained a lot of these people in these techniques, I knew the tricks of how to escape when I was being followed. They were watching me. And since I had taught a lot of them—not all, but some of them—I could keep track of them. When they had not seen or heard from me for one or two days, they would start to call the house, and this really bothered me personally because I realized that they were not respecting my family or my privacy.

My bosses started giving me jobs to do that were really simple-minded. They would say to me, "Listen, this parking attendant at such-and-such a restaurant looked the wrong way at my wife. You! Go! Put him in his place."

I mean, this was not a job for me. This was a job for a beginner. They knew that I was not the type of person who would be able to put someone in his place. My style of work was not, "Hey! Stop looking that way at so-and-so's wife," and give him a few slaps on the face. This was not a job for me, so I said, "Okay, I'll take charge. I'll order someone to do it."

But they would come back and insist, "No! *You* do it. *You* take care of it."

The problem was not that I was not capable of doing such a beginner's job. Rather, because of all of the time I had spent living and working in this circle—ever since I received my first training—from the very first time that I received the order to execute someone . . . since I had been taught to spend days guarding someone . . . since I had learned to spend thirty or sixty days in silence and closed up in a room . . . since they taught me to be under the influence of drugs and to stay awake for up to two weeks . . . since I was taught to *never ever* leave an enemy alive. . . .

All of these circles for me had only one purpose. I could no longer go and just say to this guy, or to anyone, "Look, don't be a pain in the ass." My attitude did not allow me to just say, "Hey. Stop bothering me. Go away." No. My attitude was that of a killer. My job was to carry out executions.

When I no longer had drugs or alcohol in my body, I started to see inside of myself and to reflect on my life. I said, "This is going to be forever, for my whole life." This happened to me. I go out and I can no longer just blow it off and tell the person to quit causing trouble for the boss or whoever. No, instead I get there and I hit the person or even *bam*—take out the pistol and shoot him. Just like that! Normal. I get in the car and leave, and none of this bothers me at all. And so when the boss gets upset with this, I argue, "So why are you scolding me?"

"Well, because we told you just to threaten him, not to kill him."

And I say, "No, you don't send *me* just to give a warning. You don't use *me* just to scare people. That is not what I am trained to do. If that is what you want, then go find someone who is just starting out."

I had lived through too much. The circle was closing in. This vicious circle that all of us in this life pass through, those of us who are trained and selected over the years. It is a circle, and there comes a time when you know intuitively what you have to do. If they send a certain person, it is because they know what that person is going to do. They will not send someone without knowing exactly what they are capable of doing. Even if the person is really small, the size of the person doesn't matter. The person might be taller or bigger, or smaller than you, but all are equally dangerous. What matters is that you have the wisdom and the nerve to know what to do with the person.

What happened to me at this time was that I could not control my instincts to carry out an order if it only went halfway. When they said, "We want him alive." Okay. What this meant is that we would use the complete team and equipment. All would be dressed in military uniforms, or uniforms of the federal judicial police or of the federal attorney general's office. All in black, bulletproof vests, official vehicles.

Sometimes I acted only as an observer. But if a target started to run away or escape, then the observer might have to become the executioner. You could not commit the error of stopping someone and then let him get away. You could not under any circumstances allow this to happen.

So the person with the most training is the one who would be assigned the position of watching over the entire operation. And in the case that something went wrong, the observer would be aware of what was going on, and this person who was also a good executioner would be in a position to finish the job. When the person has been shot, whether in a house or in a car, after the attack there would always be someone assigned to approach the scene alone to give the target the *tiro de gracia*, the coup de grâce. This is to secure the objective. Until this is done, the job is not finished. Even if the person is completely stitched with bullets and the body is drenched with blood, the job is not finished until it is secured. The secure job is a shot to the head, and if you want the job secured, this is what you must do.

It's a mistake when they send someone like me to do a beginner's job. It is difficult because once you have passed through all these stages of the vicious circle, you are no longer able to do just a little part of a job. It might be possible for me to do such a job if I were under the influence of the right drug or something that would calm me down, but that was not the situation for me at this time.

And it was at this critical time in my life that every day, every single day, I would see this sign along the road to my house.

IF YOU NEED HELP, DIAL THIS NUMBER. *HE* WILL HELP YOU.

Always, always, always along my way, I would be confronted by this message.

• • •

Some time went by, and I made an error. My bosses asked me to go to another city to get some money from a guy who owed the organization. I was just sent to collect. This was another humiliating, simple job for a person like me. When I got the money, I made a deposit, but I kept some of the money for myself. This money was not mine. I stole it. And I went back to *la vida loca* for a week, doing drugs and drinking. When my boss found out that I had kept some of the money that I was supposed to have deposited, he was very very upset and angry with me. The organization lost the trust that they had had in me before.

And then, while I am in this other city, I run onto that same advertisement again, but in a different form. I see this sign:

CHRIST LOVES YOU.

But I say, for me, there is no Christ.

So what happens? My bosses send people from my own team, my own group, to find me. But I was alert. I realized that people were looking for me, so I would move around every three hours or so. Since I was not a beginner, I knew that the people they had sent were not that trustworthy, not people of the highest confidence. These were people I had trained myself, and some of them owed me favors. I could ask them, "So what do you want with me? Just ask. Don't cause more problems for yourselves."

They keep following me. For a week I keep running here and there. But after a few more days I decide that I must confront them—the worst they can do is kill me. And I knew by this time that if I did not go to the meeting as ordered, these people would go after my family. So I find a telephone and make the call.

"Where do you want to meet me?"

"Meet me right here."

So I get a bus. I did not have a car by this time. I go to the place I was told to meet in this other city.

He gives a long sigh. His voice reflects this moment when he became the hunted rather than the hunter.

The trip . . . was long. For me, it seemed eternal. I was now the target. I knew I was headed for a troublesome situation, with someone very difficult. But I was not afraid. I knew I could manage it. My heart told me that I would be able to manage the situation but that there would be problems. I felt something, but it was not fear. It's not that I didn't know what it was to be afraid.

But I was not afraid. I knew that the worst thing that could happen is that they would kill me.

When I get to the meeting place, no one is waiting for me. I call again. They tell me to wait. Suddenly, two vehicles arrive out of nowhere. I am told to get in one of them. I get in and I am immediately kidnapped. Yes, I fell right into a trap. They kidnap me. Along the route I see several cars. One behind the car I am in, but no car at all in front. For almost the whole way there is a police car following behind us. It would not have cost me anything to open the car door. Since they didn't know very well how to do the job, they did not handcuff me. I got into the car voluntarily. I could have said something obscene to the driver of the police car, yelled out something and caused a distraction so that they would have had to stop us. But I knew that if I had made such a move to escape, they knew where to find my family and this would have put them in great danger.

We were en route to a safe house for nearly forty minutes—something that should not be done. From where they picked me up it should have taken no more than seven minutes to get to where they were going. They kneel me down on the floor and begin to beat me up. I felt so much anger, rage, and powerlessness in this moment. I looked at them, and I said to myself, "Lord, dear God. Why don't I just do something to get rid of them?"

There are not many of them, just five guys, and one of them stops watching me and goes into the bathroom. I could just do away with them right here. I am trained to do this. And I started crying from rage. And they started laughing at me. "Hey, man, we thought you were more of a man than this."

He chuckles a little bit wryly, remembering.

And when I'm lying there on the floor and this one guy says to me, "Hey, I thought you were more of a man," and I tell him, "You know why I am crying? Because I am afraid I will kill you. I'm crying because I am afraid that I could make mincemeat out of you all. I could tear you up with my bare hands."

And then another person comes in, and he gives me a telephone.

"Yes," I answer to the voice on the phone. And the voice answers, "You have thirty seconds to get yourself out of there."

"Okay."

"And I never want to see you again." I knew who it was that I was talking to. They take the telephone away from me, and then this same person gives the order to the others not to let me leave.

• • •

God is great. God is powerful. This other guy who had gone into the bathroom, I knew who he was. A few months ago my bosses had sent me after him. "Go, find him. He owes about $40,000. Tell him to pay up. If he doesn't give you the money, get rid of him."

When I had found him, about a month before all this happened, I grabbed the guy like I was ordered, and I said to him, "I need you to pay up. I know you have enough money. Pay what you owe. It isn't much. If you don't have it here, go get it. When you have the money, call me, pay up, and you won't have any more problems." I gave him the phone number. And I let him go. But I never saw him again until the day of my kidnapping.

By this time I was naked. I don't know where they got these guys who were supposed to be guarding me. One of them went in the kitchen, another one went out to the patio, another changed rooms, one went outside to talk on the telephone. And this one that I knew, the guy who had been in the bathroom, he comes in and he tells me, "Look, I don't have anything against you. And I don't have anything to thank you for. But you know what? I'm not one of them, and I don't take orders from them. So if you want to leave, here is the door." I looked around. None of the others were there. Just him. He had a gun. I just kept looking at him. Then I stood up, naked, opened the door, and I ran.

Just before I got to the entrance gate of the neighborhood— it was a private subdivision with a guard at the gate—a car pulls up to me with this same guy driving. Since I was naked, I was hiding under another car. And he says to me, "Come on out. The guards at the gate have orders not to let you leave. They are coming after you." And I said to myself: Why? I am going to have to do what I don't want to do.

At this moment, he is still afraid that he will have to kill again.

So I said to him, "What do I do?"

And he said, "Get in the car."

This person, who for some reason at the right moment was sent by God to give me an order that I could trust . . . this guy took me out in his car. When he dropped me off in a safe place, I went to free my wife and my daughter from the place where they were staying. I jumped over the wall in back because I knew that the people who had taken me would be watching the house. I took my wife and my daughter out of the house and we fled. I only had time to take a T-shirt and one pair of pants, that's all. I took them out and we fled. Later, the house was ransacked. They took weapons, drugs, and the cash I had there. I only had enough time to save my family.

• • •

After all of this happened, I hid for a few more days in that city, and I always remembered the sign and the telephone number. I asked myself: Why? Why? Why?

I had to leave, and I had to leave my family. I sent my family to one place while I went somewhere else. Nothing was safe now, my destiny was uncertain, we could not stay together. I did not want them to find me and take me along with my family. This was a very real danger. If they kidnapped me and my family was with me, we would all have to die alone, all of us. I thought it better to be separated. We began to run from state to state, city to city, completely separated. We never saw each other. We had no money, we had nothing, and yet, little by little, we were getting out of this prison, this life that we had been living until then. We could not get back together.

I had to travel alone, and I went to see a person who, on at least four or maybe even six occasions, I had been sent by my bosses to find and execute. But first, I had been ordered to collect more than $1.5 million that he owed. I had never been able to find this person to complete the job.

When I arrived in the other city, I got the telephone directory, and the first thing I saw was an advertisement for his company.

The person he is going to see is a man he knew who had worked for the cartel but had since become a Christian and left the criminal organization. He went to this person to ask him for help.

So I called his business and managed to make an appointment to see him. But when this man heard my name, instead of hiding or running away, what he said was, "Tell him to come right now and I will see him." That is what I did. I went there, and he received me. I know that he knew that I was the person who had been looking for him to kill him. But I had never found him until this moment.

It surprised me even more when I saw him. I went to his office, and he was very calm, as if nothing were going to happen. He gave me his hand and said, "What can I do for you?" He told me that he had been waiting for me, that something had spoken to him and told him I was coming, that I had a problem and that he had to wait for me. He then listened to me for a few minutes, and he was very attentive to what I told him. And the most ridiculous thing that could possibly happen to me is that he immediately starts talking to me about God. He talks about God and the love that He has for me. He says, "God has been looking for you for a long time. He has put signs and messages for you to see so that you will come to Him. He has already paid for your sins. You do not have to worry."

And I said, "That is impossible. They [the men from the criminal organization who had kidnapped him] are looking for me. I escaped. I ran away. They are out there looking for me. I've done this and this. I owe this. I have done all of these terrible things. . . ."

He said, "Don't worry. God is going to cleanse you. He has already washed away your sins. The fact that you are here with me, the fact that I am spending time with you. . . ."

And I tell him, "Look, you know what? I need a safe place to hide. Where is that?"

And he said, "I'm going to tell you something. No one here is going to capture you alive. Because those who know you, they know where you are coming from, they know who you are and why you are here. The only person who could possibly save you would be a crazy person."

And he said, "You know what? I am going to invite you to come with me. There is someone you need to meet." And he took me to a crazy person, *un loco*. And it was this crazy person who gave me asylum for weeks, months. But he was not just any loco. He was a person who had a whole lot of other locos around him, and they all loved him. And I began to feel the love and affection of these people who had really gone over the wall. People who had gone completely crazy and were now nothing but idiots. They had completely lost their minds. Some of them were people who had done things in their lives and repented, but God had not given them the opportunity to leave in time, like He had given me. God had given me the chance to escape in time from this vicious circle.

When the other person brought me to this loco, he said to me, "He is the only person who can help you out of this, the only one who can give you a hand. I cannot help you in any other way." He did not have any safe houses. What he did have was money—he was okay financially—and could have put me up in a hotel or a house, but that would not have been safe for me. I needed something very secure, and he said to me, "What could be more secure than to stay with this crazy person?" When I got there with this loco, he talked to me about God also.

It surprised me that after one, two, three nights went by . . . he had such patience with me. And he finally asked me, "You want to talk?" And we sat face to face in two big chairs. And I talked and talked and talked. I wasn't sleepy at all. I felt terror, desperation, desolation. I asked about my family. What is going to happen to my family? And this person said to me that if I were

there with him, if God had brought me there, it was because He had rescued me. Because God had already paid for all of my sins and I had to repent and accept Him. And in this moment all I could say was: "No. I'm here because I am lucky. They will be coming after me."

And then he says, "Let me have my way. Since I took you in, go along with me. I'm offering this to you." And he takes me again, takes me by the hand.

And he takes me to this really big place—a church or religious sect or something. It is huge. We sit in one of the rows of chairs. I turn around, and again I realize the immensity, how many men there are there. What could it be that brings thousands of men here, what is it? This was a big surprise for me. A huge number of men, crying and screaming and dancing. I know now that this was a praise service, that they were praying and praising God. But at the time I had never seen anything like it, and it made me laugh. I thought to myself, "All these faggots, crying over a song? Ugh. They are really fucked up." They were all on their feet, and it wasn't ten or twenty or thirty. It was more like 4,500 men, calling out to a God that I did not know. Crying and praising Him, telling God that they loved Him. "Ugh," I said to myself. "I'm not going to get out of this alive."

And I went back to the house where this person had given me shelter. So he asked me, "What did you think?"

"Well, they cry, they sing, they dance around," I said. "But what are they going to do if someone comes into that church looking for me? What are they going to do? They are no shelter against an AK-47. One blast from an AK-47 can go through fifteen bodies lined up just like that! Just one barrage from an AK. *Phroom!* Takes them all out. What are they gonna do? So what if there are five thousand or ten thousand. What are they going to do?"

And he answered: "Them? Nothing. It is God, the Lord, who will save you. God has some reason for you being here. He wants you for something."

The next day he had to go to the church again, and so I said, "I want to go too. I want to go see how all these faggots cry."

And he chuckles as he remembers this.

My surprise was, as soon as I got there . . . I don't know what I felt. I really can't explain this feeling. I just started to cry.

He starts to cry now as he tells the story.
Tears wash over his voice.

I did not hear the preaching, I did not hear anything. From the time I got there and the praise group started to play their first chord, I fell to crying. I cried as I had never cried, more than I

ever remember crying in my childhood. I cried from nine or ten o'clock in the morning, I don't know. I cried for five or six hours without stopping. Kneeling down, falling down on the floor. And asking God to forgive me for all that I had done.

And I heard the people crying for me, and I felt their hands touching me. I reached out to them. And in my mind I began to see all of this.

He flips back through the pages
of the notebook where he has sketched his story.

All of this that I had lived for years, in the matter of minutes or hours, it all flashed through my mind, and it was being erased from me. All of this that I had done. "Look, I did this, and this and this!"

And each time someone came close to me and touched me, I could feel the warmth of them touching me, burning away my past sins. They said, "You are free. You are free."

And I remembered, "No, I did this and this and this. . . ." They cried and they prayed. I saw myself as a child, my whole life was passing before my eyes so quickly . . . from the time I was very young, my adolescence, all of my life was passing in front of me. I saw many good things passing before me. I remembered my parents, my childhood, I remembered happy moments, I remembered the circus, I remembered my mother when she was still alive, I remembered having fun with my brothers, I remembered everything I had forgotten, I remembered each moment that I had left behind in order to go to serve a person who was not worth anything. All of these memories came to me and filled my heart with joy.

And I said, "What is this?" This is all good, this is what it is to be good, this is setting me free from this yoke, this burden, that I have been carrying on my back all this time. All of the years under the yoke of the cartels, under the yoke of these people who held me down with their foot on my neck, giving orders, giving orders. It was from all of this that I was being liberated.

These were very beautiful moments, moments in which my passion overflowed. I did not know yet at this moment that He was crying, that God Himself was crying out to me, but I realized that something extraordinary was happening. The next day they said to me, "If anyone wants to come forward to receive the Lord, come." It was automatic. I did not need to say, "Yes, I want to." I just stood up and walked toward the front. I got there, and I said a few small prayers, I said just a few little words—"Yes, I love Him, I want it, because I am feeling it, I want to belong to this family, I want to belong to Him"—because He had just given me something that no one had ever given me before, the joy of remembering how beautiful life is, how beautiful it is to be free, how beautiful it is to be with my brothers and sisters, with my family, with pleasure to be with them . . . with the family that I already knew that I had.

My emotion was so great, I said to Him, "No one, no one in this world, no one on this earth can do anything to me that my Lord Jesus Christ does not want to happen to me. From today, I am reborn in Him." I felt that each time I accepted the guilt for each of the things that I had done and that each time someone touched me, I felt that I was burning and I felt forgiveness. And from this moment I felt free from each and every one of the terrible things that I had done. Free from the errors that I had committed. I put myself in the hands of God. I asked the Lord for His forgiveness, and I accepted Him in my heart.

And in the same way I have asked God, for all of this time, for all of the people who are there, people in the criminal life, who involuntarily believe . . . to tell them, to any individual who feels grand, who dares to call himself "Lord," "*Señor*" . . . I want to tell him that the Lord is in Heaven and that He is the only One capable of miracles, that He is the only One capable of causing the rain, lightning, thunder . . . that He is the only One capable of resurrecting us and bringing us back into the world pure in spirit and to show us His beauty and love . . . that He has always been with us, but that it is we who have not given Him the opportunity to show us His love.

Those who call themselves "Señor"* are more cowardly than any other. They live in the shadows, they hide in darkness, believing that they are helping poor people in the Sierra, people who are alone and poor with nothing but the crops that they produce.

And these people feel content and feel that they are gods. There are those who call themselves "Master." But the only Mas-

---

* He is referring here to the name given to Amado Carrillo, the former head of the Juárez cartel, who was known as El Señor de los Cielos (Lord of the Skies), and to other powerful figures in the narco-trafficking organizations. In English, of course, we call these people *druglords*.

ter is in Heaven. There are those who call themselves "Master," "Boss," "Señor." But they are not worthy to speak in this manner. The only Lord that I know, the only Lord who allows me to be here, is my Lord Jesus Christ.

And to all who are able to hear this message, and who find themselves or who have gone through a situation like that that I have experienced, I tell you to call upon the Lord Jesus Christ and ask Him to help you. The Lord is for all. He is not just for one, He is for all. And he gives us salvation and eternal life. After this I can tell you, just as you see these blank pages, I know that if my life should end today I am happy. I am so happy because I know that I will go to Heaven and live with my Lord Jesus Christ. I will be with Him because he died for me. Through His wounds and His suffering, I have been forgiven and cleansed. He paid for me and for my sins. I have repented, and I am no longer afraid to die. My fears are finished. My family needs security, and my Lord will provide this security for my family. And our Lord Jesus Christ is the only One worthy of being called Lord.

He pauses for a long time.

Never be afraid. Never be afraid of anyone. No one is stronger through size or wisdom than our Lord Jesus Christ. No matter how tall or short or wide, there is no one stronger than Him. I know that there are many people who are fed up with having to live under the yoke of the boss, the *cacique*. I know that there are people who wrongly try to live for money and power. But there is no solution except to speak to the Lord of Lords, the King of Kings, who is our Lord Jesus Christ. No one in this world can reach or hope to be even a grain of sand in His hand compared to what He wants for us.

Be aware, repent, and live a life in Him.

God is good, and God loves us. God wants us to be with Him. And God forgives.

Thank you, God, for the life that You have given me.

Thank you, Lord, for the family that You have given me.

Thank you, Father, for allowing me to be here to share this with others who may also be able to be with You.

I only want to tell You that you exist, that you are good and kind.

And if You have accepted me, if You have forgiven me, then anyone, everyone, can be forgiven.

Amen.

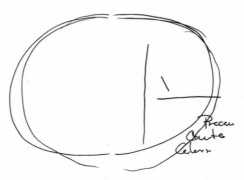

✣

THE SYSTEM
AND THE LIFE

THE LIFE, 1

A routine day. . . .

Well, let's say you get up in a hotel in Torreón. It's 6:00 A.M. Eat a quick breakfast, American-style, like they give you for free in the hotel. Wait for the people you are working for to get up since you are always dependent on their orders. Take turns at guard. When the boss gets up, go with him to eat lunch, wherever he wants to go.

Then patrol the city. Look out for new people in town, new vehicles. Be sure that there are no new people who might be working for another cartel. There are informants at the checkpoints outside of town to let you know if there are new people moving in. These informants let us know, and we go to investigate, see what they are up to. The narcos operate just like a federal or state agency. Things are coordinated. Whatever they earn, they spend.

In the evening, go to a good restaurant to eat, and then get some girls for the boss. Check to make sure the girls are happy, that everybody is satisfied with the hotel.

From there go to a safe house. You want to know what these places are like? So, here we are. We feel safe, more or less, but you are never sure whether something has happened in this place before. The less you know the better. You go from safe house to safe house. Was someone killed there? Are bodies buried here? There are very few people who know which places have been used as cemeteries. Not all of these places are used to kill people or bury people.

Fear? It's not really fear, but the main thing is that you just forget about it. Under the influence of drugs and alcohol, you really are not afraid. You can always sense nervousness and fear, you can smell fear in another person, and if you do, if a person hesitates or shows fear or nervousness, you have to get rid of him, because he could cause the whole operation to fail.

Once you do something, forget about it! There are executions that take place in a matter of seconds. You have to do the work as if it comes natural to you. Take care of the job, hide the vehicles, change clothes, go to a fine restaurant, natural. If you cannot, you cannot do the work, and you are likely to become one of the statistics, one of the many who are executed.

The drugs help a lot. They especially help when you need to stay awake for a long time. But even the drugs have their limit. Sometimes it is good to get high, to get in the right state of mind

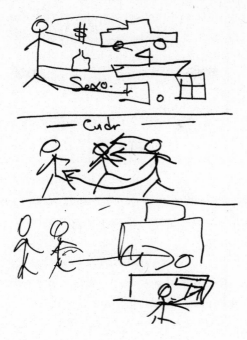

to do certain work, but it is better not to be high on drugs all the time. No one wants to be guarded by someone who is always doing drugs.

When you are living the wild life, *la vida loca*, when you have money, liquor, women and sex, cars . . . you can enjoy yourself on a yacht. You have houses and apartments. They don't belong to you, but you can use them whenever you want. Because they facilitate the work.

You do not just become addicted to the money, the sex, the liquor and the drugs, but you get to the point where you really like all of this stuff. There are times, during the nights when you can really sleep well . . . but those nights are few. Really, you don't often get the sleep that you need to take care of yourself or to maintain your personal integrity. But sometimes, when you do sleep, you realize that in the same group of three or more people this one is capable of pulling out a knife and killing another, and you realize that if that is the case he might be capable of killing you too. This is just to say that you always have to watch out for yourself.

The horrible thing is when you are dreaming. You have very realistic dreams. I would dream that I was running through the streets, jumping over cars. Oh, I would dream that I was out there and did not have my weapon and they were chasing me. And the dreams were so real that I would wake up and the gun was on the pillow and I would have my weapon in my hand and I would be aiming it.

I was very violent. The dreams are not things that could never happen, they are not fantastic dreams, but very realistic. The fear that I had that kept me from sleeping in my house with my family, the reason I would go someplace to sleep by myself—and this is a very real fear and it happened to the majority of people in this situation—it was because the least little noise would cause you to react violently. If your wife comes to the bedroom, if she touches you, your head is full of such terrible things from this world that it is about to explode. And you can react and cause her harm.

One time my wife tried to help me when I was dreaming. She felt how I was sweating and calling out in my sleep . . . *Ah, ah, ah*. She saw I was having a nightmare and tried to wake me up, but when she touched me—*ARRRGGH*—my reaction was to grab her by the throat, but I didn't wake up in time and my hands were on her throat, I was strangling her, I was strangling my own wife!

And from that moment, that very moment, I realized that

something very bad was happening to me. I was no longer any good. There was a line that I had respected between the work I did—as a guard, as an instructor, as an executioner—but this work no longer stayed on one side of the line. Now it had passed over into my life at home. I could no longer control my instinct to be violent and aggressive. I could no longer tell the difference between this world and that of my own family. You even start to think that your own family is against you and you can do harm to your own family.

When I saw the fear in her face, and to have my own wife paralyzed and defenseless in my own hands, unable to move . . .

He pauses, sobs and gasps for breath,
and then resumes telling the story.

. . . It caused me to stop sleeping at my house for a long time. It is difficult to sleep with someone when you are so deep into this element. It is hard to share this with anyone.

This is not an excuse to say, "Just find an easy woman to sleep with. . . ." Really, you know that if you are capable of doing this in your own home, you know it could happen with another person also. And I do not have any doubt that at times when there is a crime and people go into motel rooms and find someone strangled, that it was caused by this stress that people are living with and the person did not realize it in time and someone was killed.

It is an instinct that gets out of control—your actions no longer belong to you. I'm not saying it is an animal instinct, rather, it is a logical reaction. If you attack me, I'm not going to wait for you to hit me again. I had been trained, and my job was to be the person who always wins. Even if someone attacks me first, as long as the attack is not successful the first time, I'm not going to allow the person to attack me twice or even touch me a second time. I am going to eliminate him. I cannot wait, because I will never leave an enemy alive to strike me again.

THE SYSTEM, 1

During the time that we were being trained as elements inside of the academy, they make a selection. In each class, they select five men who have the best averages. And these police-in-training have the opportunity to travel to Tucson, Arizona, to an FBI training center. It is a short training session, three days. The first day they teach about the hidden serial numbers for tracking stolen vehicles. They show us how vehicles not only have serial numbers in the usual places but also hidden numbers located on different parts of the vehicle, such as the motor or the chassis, and also vehicles that are coming out with serial numbers on the windows. This is the first day.

On the second day, they gave us more training in the techniques of arrests and follow-up investigations. They showed us a little more of their technology, how to locate people using their fingerprints. The system that they have is very large, and they can detect one person in the world by his fingerprints because of the huge database that they have.

The third day is very relaxing and nice. After breakfast, they take us for a time to a firing range and give us a tour of the facilities, but only a part of it. They don't show us the whole installation—the different laboratories, dormitories, firing ranges. In comparison to an academy in Mexico where we are studying, these facilities are really something. When you get to a training facility of the FBI, you are surprised at how big the installation is. It is like a whole city.

In the afternoon, after lunch, this is the last day, and they take us to relax, maybe to a bar, for those who want to drink a beer or something. We talk and tell stories and get to know each other. Usually there is one of our instructors from the academy and three or four FBI agents with us the whole time. There are always people guarding us even though we are invited guests. We always have a guide, a minder, they never leave us on our own. That's just the way they do it. It is part of the training and military-type instruction that they give us.

What they don't ever seem to know is that among the five elements receiving this training, it is very possible that two or three or at a minimum one of them is already receiving money from banks in the United States, money that comes from the narco-

trafficking organizations. And the narcos are paying for this police cadet to get this beneficial training from the FBI.

After these three days are over, we return to the academy in
a bus to resume our normal instruction.

• • •

All of the time that we are in the academy—six months—we are
learning about laws, forms of arrest, how to follow up investigations. But that's not all. The school is also a base for learning
about corruption, starting with the process of buying off the
guards at the entrance gates so that we can escape the academy
and have some time to relax. Even better when one is getting payment from the outside.

Many times some of us compared this kind of lockup to
being in prison. There isn't much difference because in the prisons
in Mexico, if you have enough money, you can pay and have a
night out to have fun. You pay off a couple of guards, go out and
have fun, and come back the next day. In the academy, it's the
same, except that here you aren't detained for a crime, rather, you
are in the academy to receive training to fight crime. The government never knows—well, they know, but they never fully
acknowledge—that of one hundred elements training in the
academy, about sixty of them will be fighting against the other
forty because those sixty are being paid for and trained by the
mafia, by the narco-trafficking organizations.

It isn't that they are not teaching morale or principles. We all
salute the flag and stuff. But the vision of the person is nothing
more than just being there. I am sure that of the one hundred elements that are admitted to the police academy, ninety of them
go in with the idea that when you are in the police, you can make

money. In the police, there is money thanks to corruption. There are ways to get bribes, *la mordida*, there are ways to make money dealing in stolen goods, *trabajar chueco*. In the police, there are always lots of ways to make money.

The salary of a policeman or an investigator is nothing. Every two weeks while I was in the academy, I would get half of the salary of an active-duty policeman. Their salary then was 300 pesos, so I would get 150 pesos while in training. That was nothing compared to the $1,000 they sent me from outside so that I would be well taken care of. The narcos invest a lot of money in their people, who will be well trained to work for them and wage the war from the inside for the cartels.

THE LIFE, 2

It is like being an addict. The addict needs to have his shot every day. When the day comes and the addict refuses his shot, he is no longer any use to the criminal organization because he is no longer going to be a consumer. He is no longer going to do what he had to do before to get his shot. When an addict reforms, he goes through a struggle. But when he reforms, he starts to believe in his principles, in his own personality and character, and he begins to see his way of life from a different point of view. And he begins to realize the things he has done. He begins to dream and to hallucinate and to see the filthy things that he did under the influence of the drugs. Things that he had forgotten. And he realizes that he has committed many errors.

This makes the other people lose trust in those who have been able to overcome their addiction. Why? Not because they cannot trust the person, but because now they themselves are seen as lesser people, as weaker people, than those who have been able to overcome their addiction. They then have to constantly fight to maintain their place of confidence and their position in the organization. The highest bosses almost never use drugs. They might get high sometimes, but they are not regular users. It is not permitted.

It serves them to have the drug users working below them because it helps them to be able to do the work. I read an article that said something I think is true. . . . How can you kill a person and not have awareness of what you are doing? Well, it is like being drunk. A person under the influence of drugs has a different awareness of things. A person uses drugs to speed things up. But once a person stops using, he has a different awareness, and it is not so easy to do certain things. Of course not. It might cause the person to be afraid and hesitate, and then the team would go after him, try to get rid of him. It is a dangerous situation.

Now, for me, to stop using alcohol and drugs was never a problem. I stopped using various times for long periods. But it was a big problem for my bosses, it was a problem of trust. So what did I have to do at times? I would see that they were nervous about me.

The time comes—I've told you before and I will tell you again—when God needs something from you, and in this moment you are in God's hands. It is through the Hand of God that you do what you do, it is not due to fear or nervousness or the influence of drugs. You are in danger and God is cleansing you, He is shaking you down, He is controlling what happens to you, and He is using the dangerous situation to make you understand what you must do.

It was during these times that I moved around a lot. Jumping from place to place, I became aware of the Hand of God, and how He would not leave me alone. And how was this possible for me, since I had by this time lost all the money I had? Both the narcos and the authorities were looking for me. How could I travel from place to place unless the Lord was watching over me and keeping me safe? How could I get across borders? With God, I could go anywhere. These are what you call miracles! And when miracles happen, you take notice.

These things were happening against my will because God was washing me clean. You see? God was taking away all of the vices and all of the evil things that I had lived. The drugs and alcohol I had left behind before, but things changed so much in me that my bosses lost confidence in me, and they sent people to hunt me down and kill me. . . .

What happened? God called me, He took me out of there. He watched over me and put people in my path to guide me to Him. And I broke down in the presence of the Spirit of God. And I thank Him for allowing me to live. This is the only Lord, my God, that I respect and serve now. There is no other power greater than the power of God.

And now the narcos have more reasons to worry about me. Many of them are atheists or they worship Santa Muerte* or some other cult. And now they fear me because I'm not just some crazy guy that stopped doing drugs. Now I am a crazy guy who is protected by the power of God. For God there are no borders. I am a living example of what God can do. He has taken me from

---

* La Santa Muerte (Saint Death), or La Santisima (Most Holy Death), is a sacred figure venerated by many in Mexico, especially in areas where criminal gangs are most prevalent. See Steven Gray, "Santa Muerte: The New God in Town," *Time*, October 16, 2007.

place to place. I have a global passport, *gracias a Dios*, thanks be to God.

• • •

Throughout all of this that I have told you, the reality is that you are not really working as a policeman or an agent. All you really are is a puppet, *un monigote*. You are manipulated and controlled, your actions are controlled for the convenience of the boss, *El Patron*. And you rise according to how well you perform your job. And as you learn to perform your job better, you begin to earn a higher salary. And these salaries are fat and juicy. And one thing that you learn right away is that this money is easy come and easy go.

You can have a lot of weapons, uniforms, and cash stored and guarded in a warehouse, but in one moment, if you fall out of favor with the boss, he can take it all away from you. And the only one who gains is the boss. He can take away your life, and he can take away your family.

• • •

These numbers are very important, very representative.

He points back to the drawings he made
of the houses used for clandestine burials.

One hundred persons. Can you imagine one hundred people buried in a cemetery, but they are piled one on top of another? Can you imagine trying to identify, trying to recognize those people? Can you imagine in a one-hundred-twenty-square-meter lot, ten meters by twenty meters, that there are fifty people buried in a common grave? Can you imagine how it is possible that

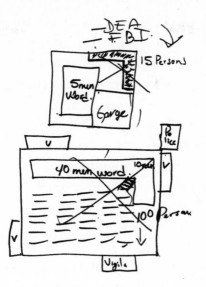

when a clandestine cemetery comes to light and the news media are notified and they arrive to cover the story, that armed men show up to intimidate them, and they tell the reporters: "Get out of here right now or this is where you will end up too."

Who has the power? Try to imagine who has the power in this kind of government. When all of the open spaces, the back roads, and the streets are guarded and patrolled by the Army. So, who is allowing all of the drugs to pass? Who is able to do this? If anyone unauthorized tries to pass drugs through, they are eliminated.

Well, those who have been trained with them for years, from a policeman with a career, from the street cop to the soldier—all of them have been trained for years to work under the command of the narcos. And the narco is a cartel. And it is a cartel that is fighting using the same police that the government has provided. Fighting for the plaza, to control territory.

And the only person who never realizes that he is dying is the puppet, *el monigote*, the person they have hanging here. For trying to be faithful, this person who has made just one mistake, they are going to chase him down and burn him to death in a barrel of boiling water, and they will make him suffer until he begs for mercy, until he begs for a bullet. And the people there will laugh at him.

You know what I want to tell you? I want to serve as an example for the rest. I can be an example, but I am only one of many. You could find ten more just like me.

THE SYSTEM, 2

In the Mexican justice system . . . here, I'm going to show you.

He begins to draw another schematic. . . .

This is the presidency, and these are the states. And each state has a governor. But I can assure you. . . . That is, I cannot tell you for certain that the president is mixed up in everything, but I can assure you that the people just below him, in his administration, many of them are bought and paid for by the narco-trafficking organizations.

And so these safe houses exist all over Mexico. And I can tell you that in terms of the border—Nogales, Tijuana, Juárez, and even small towns like Ojinaga—there are houses where the federal judicial power and the government leaders and those in the Secretariat of *Gobernación* [*Interior*],* which is the strong arm of the Presidency of the Republic, where they know that people are buried. Not one or two or three or four . . . but more than three hundred, maybe four hundred people. I can't tell you exactly who they are or what their names are. That is difficult. One cannot know everything. But in the day-to-day work that we did, I can tell you that of the forty, fifty, maybe even one hundred people who were kidnapped, that there are no more than five or six left alive. The rest of them will never be found. And these government people have knowledge of all of these safe houses.

And I can tell you, for example, of this house where thirty-eight people are buried, or of another one where maybe eighty people are buried. There are police squad cars guarding these houses, parked at strategic places on the nearby streets. Because they are being paid to protect these places so that these bodies never see the light of day.

In places where they have discovered bodies in different cities, this has happened because the FBI or the DEA has pressured the

---

* This is the cabinet-level government department in charge of internal security.

Mexican government to uncover these places. But the reality is that they know that there are informants for the DEA or the FBI buried there. There are people who had worked as informants, and they ended up buried in these places.*

I can tell you one important bit of information: These informants of the DEA, it is no longer a good idea to bury them, because they now wear a chip, a computer tracking chip, that was not used before. And now all of the DEA informants in Mexico have these chips, and even though they are buried, the problem is that they can be located quickly using a GPS satellite system, and that system is global.**

The narco-traffickers know this. In the past they would use a scanner to try to determine if a person was wearing a chip, but they are really small and are usually implanted in the neck or in the hand. But now they do not always know where they are implanted. And so some of these informants who were wearing chips ended up buried, and because of this, some of the graves have been located and excavated. But I can also tell you that some people in the DEA who were also working for the narcos informed them that these chips were giving precise locations as to where these people had been buried.

---

* The sicario is referring here to discoveries of *narcofosas*, clandestine mass graves, in several houses in Juárez in 2004 and 2008. Other narcofosas come to light periodically, not only in Juárez but in other Mexican cities and rural areas.

** It is common now for the wealthy in Mexico to have tracking chips implanted as an anti-kidnapping measure. The U.S. DEA will not provide any information on its procedures for confidential informants, but in December 2010 one of the U.S. diplomatic cables released by Wikileaks revealed that more than sixty FBI or DEA contacts had been targeted and murdered in Mexico by narco-trafficking groups. See *http://wikileaks.ch/cable/2009/01/09MEXICO193.html*. This information appeared in many national and international news media.

These are some of the reasons that I can say with confidence that the government is aware of all of this, that they know these things. The government knows that there are many people who are being instructed and trained and managed by the government for many years and that these people are then being used by the narcos. The government knows what is happening. The reason that this has not been stopped is because this system is convenient for them. There are several things about it that suit their interests.

One of these is that a certain amount of instability is advantageous to them because it enables them to keep on stealing. When really big things happen in the country, what do they do? For instance, when a guerrilla war broke out in Chiapas, the narcos took advantage of this. When there is a guerrilla war in the southern part of the country, it becomes easier to traffic drugs here in the north of Mexico. And as the trafficking increased, the cartels just grew and grew and grew. And these people in Mexico City, the generals down there in those mansions where they live? It is the same police who work for them, the same police themselves who are moving the drugs. Maybe not always in the same vehicles, but in any case, they provide the escorts for the drugs so that everything passes safely.

The government of the United States tries to be sure that its image is clean. But at the international bridges there are elements that, I can assure you, will charge, for example, $50,000 to let a Suburban pass, loaded to the gills, packed with everything it can carry, and they will not search it. And there have been investigations that have affected Mexico, and there have been global news stories in which the United States says that the narcos have not infiltrated their organizations. Well, they have, but in the United States they at least make an effort to stop this corruption. But in

Mexico they don't even try. What they do in Mexico is to give the advantage to the narcos. The government assigns forces to them, and they train and assist all of the elements that then go on to work directly for the narco-trafficking organizations.

These are logistics and things that you have to understand. What does the government do? They pay the police a small salary, but the police understand that this little salary is nothing compared to what they will earn from the narcos. You have to take into account that of all the training academies in Mexico, the most prestigious are those of the Mexican Army. And you must understand how the army's reputation was tarnished when General Rebollo was arrested and sentenced by a military court and continues to be imprisoned for having very close links with the Lord of the Skies, Amado Carrillo.*

When General Rebollo was arrested, he left very very powerful people in charge. He was the chief of intelligence in Mexico and of the army. He was the chief of the army when the president gave him this high position and power, and at the same time General Rebollo was an intimate compadre of the most powerful narco-trafficker in the country.

So what can you expect? If the highest destructive force in your country, the most powerful institution in the country—the Mexican Army—is mixed up in the narco-trafficking, what is a

---

* General Jesus Gutierrez Rebollo was Mexico's top anti-narcotics officer under President Zedillo. He was arrested in February 1997 and charged with working with drug trafficker Amado Carrillo Fuentes. Rebollo had access to all of Mexico's classified drug enforcement information, police records, and informants, which authorities believe he made accessible to Carrillo. See "Family Tree" at the PBS *Frontline* website, *http://www.pbs.org/wgbh/pages/frontline/shows/mexico/family/genrebollo.html*. For more on the career of General Rebollo, see the introduction to this book.

simple citizen supposed to do? Do you think a citizen is going to have confidence in the municipal police? The rural police? The investigative police? Or a policeman of the people who rides a bicycle and instead of a pistol carries a little wooden club? What is the citizen to do when the army arrives along with several narcos armed with AK-47s, with FAL [*Fusil Automatique Léger,* a light automatic rifle made in Belgium] or with assault rifles, or a semi-automatic machine gun, with Uzis or with weapons that can be under water and still fire? And now they are even using Barretts, weapons that can penetrate an armored vehicle. What is the population supposed to think? What can a policeman expect when a narco asks the question: "What do you want? Silver or lead? *Plata o plomo?*" Either you take the money we offer and join us, or you die. What do you do? What do you do when the whole country is invaded, infiltrated completely?

President Calderón has a very serious problem. There are informants for the narco organizations inside of his government, and he is not going to be able to clean this up. There are people there who have been corrupted for years. Calderón has not understood how other governments have dealt with this. He is favoring one cartel, and the other is going to wage war. Calderón is not going to be able to resolve this situation in one presidential term. *Ojala!* God willing! Things may get better. But it has to be cleaned up from inside the presidency.

It used to be that the army was respected in Mexico. But now putting the army in the streets puts them in the position of the police. And police are not respected. No one respects the police because everyone considers them just like they do the narcos. The army is degraded now that they are in the streets. The army is not set up to do investigations or to fight the narco-traffickers.

They are not facing a guerrilla. A lot of the weapons that the narcos themselves are using come from the army. Along the borders there is a lot of trafficking in weapons. And the weapons pass through customs, but in reality all of the border crossings are under the control of the army, and so the weapons could not get into the hands of the narcos without the army knowing about it.

Before, the army was very highly respected in Mexico. The people used to be thrilled to see a military parade, to see the weapons that only the military would have. But that was before, not now. Now, when there are searches and confiscations, they capture weapons in the hands of the narcos that are much more powerful than those used by the army.

For a long time, the army did not show up except for parades or when there was some kind of disaster in the country, like a flood or epidemic, and the federal government would call in the army to do relief work. But later, there were infiltrations by very high-level people. For example, it was known that the Lord of the Skies had people who had infiltrated the military, people who had gotten very close to the top. The military had always been very cautious. Not the whole army, but elements of the army began. . . . It is really a shame that the institution has been so corrupted, it is a shame what is happening now. Many people joined the army because they really wanted to serve the country, but they have ended up in the streets. They have been corrupted, and they are now serving the narcos. Sometimes they do not even know which side they are working for.

Before, the army would never have been in the streets, except for some very secret operations when they were called in to assist the federal police. These were very secret, very special operations. But the army would never have been called in to guard a plaza or to get mixed up in violence between cartels. The army existed to protect the sovereignty of the country. But now? Are they protecting the sovereignty? No, now they are just another instrument. They have ruined the vision of the military from what it was before. Even though the army had been involved before—after all, it was proven that General Rebollo worked for the Juárez cartel. But these things were known and not talked about, not written about in the press. But now the army is called in to get involved in the fight between the Juárez cartel and the Sinaloa cartel.

• • •

I am not going to tell you that there are no good people. There are good people in the very upper echelons of the government, from the president's own sphere, who have tried to do things right, who have tried to make it so that things function in a proper way. But these people have been destroyed. There are people who have fallen very recently. For example, Mr. Vasconcelos.* His airplane crashed, but it was not a crash caused by human error, as reported in the media. And with him, the secretary of Gobernación [*Interior*] was also killed. And he was an intimate friend of the current president of Mexico.

What I am telling you is plain to see. It was an airplane crash, and it happened because Vasconcelos and this secretary of Gobernación were working to break these links with the narco-traffickers, people that were following this line. And in the trajectory of Vasconcelos, you can understand this by looking at what he did.

---

* On José Luis Santiago Vasconcelos and Juan Camilo Mouriño, see the introduction to this book.

He talks very fast, he is pounding his pen onto the paper. . . .
His voice breaks with emotion. He is angry.

So what happened? Vasconcelos was one of the public pros-
ecutors who was involved in the largest number of excavations
of bodies in the safe houses all over the country. He had the
strength and the courage to talk to the FBI and the DEA. And
state by state, he went to people he could trust and dug up the
bodies, dug up the bodies, dug up the bodies . . . *sacó cuerpos enterrados, sacó cuerpos enterrados, sacó cuerpos enterrados.*

• • •

I haven't followed too carefully the policies of President Calderón,
but I have noticed that he has changed tactics for handling the
situation. He has tried to purge, to purify, the high ranks of his
government. Calderón has said, "I have my right arm and my
left, and I'm going to purge my right arm." But when we look at
the people that he has purged, what it looks like is that he is re-
moving the people who work for one cartel simply to replace
them with those who are part of another cartel. This is what it
looks like to people—that he is receiving payment from one cartel to get rid of those in his government who are associated with
another cartel.

Many times, not even the president of the Republic can keep
track of everything that is going on. So he has various leaders
who work for him as the secretaries of the various government
ministries and departments. For example, as I've mentioned to
you, his secretary of Interior [Juan Camilo Mouriño] was assassinated. Well, he was killed in a plane crash, and they say that
turbulence caused it. Illogical! When someone starts to do a good
job, it gets noticed, and so there are repercussions.

It is most likely that the target was not the secretary, but it was Señor Vasconcelos who was traveling with him. You go and check into who he was and what he did. See how much trouble he caused inside of the attorney general's office, even though he did not have a high post there. He was just a middle-level investigator, but he accomplished more than many other investigators with more power than he had. Just take a look at how many little bodies came crawling out of the ground because of the efforts of Señor Vasconcelos!

• • •

This situation did not in any way benefit Mexico. So what did this mean? It meant that at the highest spheres of government, there were people mixed up in the narco-business. And if everyone was involved, there came a moment when a group of high-level agents in various states had to flee because of the discovery of bodies in bunkers that they maintained for the purpose of burying people. There are really good people who try to make a difference. Unfortunately, with the corruption coming from the top, it is very hard to clean this up.

There are strategies on the part of the government—for example, they send elements of the Mexican Army to Pakistan and Spain to receive instruction in how to combat terrorism. But some of these are elements that will in turn use the military and counterterrorism instruction they receive to train the narco-trafficking groups to counter actions that the government might try to use against them.

• • •

Now I want to talk about a very powerful group in Mexico known as the Zetas. Remember, as it is said, it takes a Zeta to kill a Zeta. And a Zeta is trained to kill sixteen men without using a single weapon, he is trained to kill with his bare hands. He has the power and the training and capability to do this.*

When you have access to and control over this kind of information, you realize that the barriers have been crossed, the lines have been erased. You realize that Mexico is no longer just a place for drugs from other places to cross over into the United States. Rather, Mexico is now a producer of drugs. And it intends to displace other producers. And at the same time as the United States reinforces its borders, the introduction of drugs into the United States is decreasing. So the narcos now are trying to addict the children in the schools in Mexico. They are now working to hook people who work in the *maquiladoras* [*factories*]. And they are recruiting women to distribute drugs.

And so what is happening is the explosion of drug use in Mexico. Mexico has now passed from being an exporter and transporter of drugs and is now a consumer country. Now you can see people begging in the streets, people selling gum at intersections, people passed out in the streets, people robbing old women to get money to supply their drug habits. And where will all these people go when they try to reform themselves? All of the

---

*   The Zetas are a paramilitary criminal organization in Mexico. The original Zetas were highly trained members of a Mexican Army special forces unit who deserted to go to work for the Gulf cartel. Members of this unit received training from the U.S. School of the Americas and may also have incorporated Guatemalan special forces trained by the CIA. The Zetas now operate as an independent drug-trafficking organization in different regions of Mexico and include corrupt former federal, state, and local police officers.

people begging in the streets are completely rejected by society. There is no place for them, except for these shelters, these Christian shelters.

And these people when they leave the shelters and end up in prison [*CERESO, Centro de Readaptación Social* (Center for Social Rehabilitation)] because they have committed robberies, and they are declared mentally ill, the only thing left is to send them back to a shelter. Because the government which instructed and trained people in their schools and academies, the government that trained elements who are then handed over to work for the narcos, they then end up in charge of all these people who are thrown away because they are no longer capable of productive work.

• • •

What is it that is not convenient for the government? Why doesn't the government do anything to stop this?

Because the government is involved in the billions of dollars that are made in this business.

The government does not want a solution. What are they saying now about the government of Mexico? That the government is taking action, using the army to resolve this problematic situation. But the situation is that the power of the narco-trafficking organizations has overtaken the power of the government. The narcos will not allow the government to control them.

The president of Mexico says, "I am in control. I will control this using my army." But the degree of corruption is so high that it cannot be brought under control. What has happened is that it is now the narcos who are controlling the president.

You can point to other parts of this situation. There was an attempt on the life of Governor Reyes Baeza of Chihuahua. They killed one of the governor's bodyguards.* Of course, this was not reported as it actually happened. Do you think that only the bodyguard was killed? So what really happened? The governor gave thanks for the work his faithful bodyguard did to defend him because he knew that it was only because of this honest man doing his job that he was saved.

But there were serious errors, serious mistakes committed. From all that I have told you and from what I know from my experience, you have to realize that when people are sent to take out a particular objective, that is what they must do and there cannot be any errors. I can tell you that those who carried out this attack on the governor of Chihuahua and failed to do it properly, I know that these people are no longer alive. They have been killed because they failed to do their job and they cannot be left alive. They died for failing to do a good job.

• • •

---

* The following account is from Diana Washington Valdez, "Chihuahua Governor's Bodyguard Slain," *El Paso Times*, December 23, 2009: Mexican authorities are investigating Sunday's slaying of one of Chihuahua Gov. Jose Reyes Baeza Terrazas' bodyguards and death threats against Juarez Mayor Jose Reyes Ferriz. The governor called a news conference near midnight Sunday to provide some details about the attack in Chihuahua City that killed one of his guards, Alejandro Chaparro Coronel, and wounded two others. He said one of the armed men who allegedly killed Chaparro also was taken to a hospital with injuries. The Chihuahua governor, who drove his own vehicle with the bodyguards behind him, said he did not know whether the attack was against him or stemmed from a traffic-related dispute between his guards and the armed suspects. "We cannot speculate and will comment only about what we know," the governor said. The Juarez mayor increased his security after he and his family received death threats following Friday's resignation of ex-Juarez police chief Roberto Orduna Cruz, city spokesman Sergio Belmonte said.

And what about that job that was done years ago that I told you about, the murder of the newspaper columnist, Dr. Oropeza? Why, after the passage of so many years, have they not been able to solve this case? People have written hundreds of articles about this case. People claim to know who did it.

I know who did it.

The order came from "El Cora." El Cora assigned a team of five people to do the job. Of these people, in this moment, I know that one is in prison for other minor crimes, and he was directly involved in this murder. And there is another person also. There are two of the five who committed this crime who are alive. Why hasn't anyone done anything? Why do the Mexican authorities try to blame scapegoats who are detained in prisons in the United States? Why bother with bringing them here to charge them with this crime when they know who really did it? When there are two people here in prison and many people know it. Why doesn't anyone talk to them? Why doesn't anyone ask them what really happened? Why does another one go free? It is not just that this journalist got involved with the narcos.* When you review the articles that he wrote, you will realize that he was one of the first journalists who spoke out about the corruption and the links between the Mexican government and the narcos. And that is why he was killed. He was a great man.

It is a disgrace that the good men and the good journalists are the ones who fall. Here in the border, there have been a lot

---

* The sicario is referring to the common assumption that if a journalist is killed it is because he has been corrupted by one criminal group or another. The police, the general public, and even fellow journalists in Mexico will make this assumption and spin any investigation into the murder in the direction of establishing the "dirty" connections of the person who has been killed.

who have fallen. Every day there are more. It is not that there are not honest people. It is not that there are not honest journalists who write the truth and who have the courage to do it. There are, but they have to hide. They have to write anonymously.

People will say: "Why are you afraid if you are a journalist? Why don't you speak openly and use the power of what you write? Why don't you write the truth? You are a journalist. You should show your face and stand by what you write." But those who have shown their faces have ended up dead, and their families have ended up in the street. Their families have ended up with nothing. The government has nothing but shame. They know that these journalists have been killed. The government does nothing to help them, and their families are left with nothing.

The crime against Dr. Oropeza dates back to the years when the buildup in the power of the narco-trafficking organizations was just beginning. It was when the narcos started to contract specialized teams to carry out executions. This was the beginning of a "boom." It was a time when it did not matter what social class you came from or who you were. The fact was, even if you were a journalist or some other important person in the society, your position would not protect you. If you did anything to attack any narco-trafficker, they were going to retaliate against you, and it did not matter to them how far things went. This was at the time when the narcos were saying, "I can go anywhere and I can do anything."

And way back then, if the authorities were not able to solve such a simple crime like the murder of Oropeza, what can you expect now? This boom was something that was heard worldwide. This homicide case was dealt with all the way up to the United Nations, and yet it still could not be solved. Nothing was ever done to punish those responsible. If that is what happens with such an important case, what can a common ordinary citizen expect in these times of threats and the wave of violence that is happening today? The case of Dr. Oropeza was just a taste of what was to come. We see what is happening now.

People say, "Okay, the violence is growing and growing. These crimes are never going to end." But it is not happening by chance—it is being controlled. What happened back then was not an experiment. Rather, it was a warning. The narcos were sending out a warning to the government and to the people: that they were in control and that they could do anything. They were capable, and they had people who were very well trained, and it was the government itself that provided the people and the training to carry out any kind of job. And above all, they provided the resources to do the work, thanks to the money generated by the narco-traffickers.

That is what the murder of Dr. Oropeza meant.

• • •

Now about Vasconcelos. . . . He was a person who was very well respected right up until the moment of his death. He was respected even inside the cartels. When he began an investigation, it became a priority even to the cartels. They moved aside and gave him the space to work and to investigate. He was an upright person, very straight. He did not get mixed up in problems. And Vasconcelos is talked about because at a given moment, inside of the current government of Calderón, if they were able to have confidence in anyone, it was in him. He was supportive, respected, very well organized in his thoughts and in his words. Men like him no longer exist inside the government.

Unfortunately, what happened to him that day in the private airplane he was traveling in together with the secretary of the

Interior [*Gobernación*], well, the government says that it was an accident caused by negligence on the part of the pilots. I have known a lot of pilots . . . and despite the government's investigations, I can practically assure you that this was not an accident.

Vasconcelos carried out a lot of investigations. The majority of them were done in close cooperation with the United States. He was doing his job for the government of Mexico, but his actions indicated that he was also an important link with United States law enforcement, and he was carrying out orders based on the information provided by the United States. For example, in one of the cases he investigated, some bodies were dug up from a house. The information came from DEA in the United States, and so something had to be done about it. If the information got into his hands, he would investigate, he would act. There was a sense of security that if Vasconcelos said he would do something, he would follow through on it. This was a certainty. He was not like many other high commanders of the police or other high-level law enforcement officials in Mexico—stuck between a rock and a hard place [*entre la espada y la pared*].

And up to now there has not been another person like him. We are talking about a person who took action. He could have been blocked perhaps, but once certain information was released, his investigations could no longer be covered up. Once the reports got into his hands, it was something real, and he could not be stopped. He followed through on all of the cases he investigated. He would not give up on a case even when he was ordered to. He always followed through. He was an honorable person, a person with a clear idea of where he was going and what he was doing. And he could be trusted. Now there are no public servants like him. If in some given moment the Mexican government had been willing and able to provide him with real security, listened to his advice, and adopted some of his investigative methods, it is possible that Mexico would not now be experiencing such high levels of violence.

But what was the government going to do with a person who had this kind of knowledge? They could place him in a very high position in the government so that he would be able to direct all of the police forces under Calderón. For example, he could have been put into a position similar to that held many years earlier by Commander Ruvalcaba,* who served as a link with United States law enforcement. He was a key person. I have no doubt that in the same manner, even after Vasconcelos was transferred from the attorney general to the department of Interior [*Gobernación*], he continued acting as an important link with the U.S. He could have followed through with his investigations. But— and this is talked about a lot—what the government did instead was to degrade his position and lower his rank. And they put him directly into the line of fire. They took away the protection that he had.

He was a humble man, dedicated to his work and to his family. I would like to have met him, but I never had the chance. I heard him talked about a lot, and everyone always spoke well of him. Once, when we were in Monterrey, he was going to be there carrying out an investigation. And we were asked to leave the plaza so that he would be able to do what he needed to do. It was

---

* Commander José Refugio Ruvalcaba was a high-level officer in the Chihuahua state police. He also served as an informant for the DEA for at least seven years, providing information about the Juárez cartel to his contacts in the U.S. agency. In November 1994, he and two of his sons were killed, their bodies left inside a car parked midway on one of the international bridges between Juárez and El Paso. See Charles Bowden, *Down by the River: Drugs, Money, Murder, and Family* (New York: Simon & Schuster, 2002), pp. 41–42.

never possible for the narcos to make an arrangement with him. That is, it was better for us, the cartel operatives at the time, to just withdraw from the plaza, let him do what he was going to do, and then leave. After that, we could return and carry on with our work. I am sure that the narco bosses at the time knew what kind of investigation he was working on, because there were various infiltrators. There were people from the PGR [*Procuraduria General de la República, the federal attorney general*] or from military intelligence inside the cartels, just as the cartels had people bought and paid for inside the government.

But there was no way for the narcos to get to Vasconcelos. He was a respectable person. Perhaps he had his weaknesses, but as far as I know, he was never corrupted. He was a person of confidence. In fact, many of the narco bosses in Mexico wanted to work with him because they knew he was a man who kept his word. But this is something that Calderón did not understand how to use to his advantage.

So, it was one of those things. . . . Perhaps Calderón made a mistake. Certainly, from my perspective, my personal opinion is that the action taken was a mistake. Vasconcelos could have done more. He could have shown the way, opened things up through his investigations. Based on the real facts obtained through his investigations, many more people could have been arrested and put in prison. And without so much violence and bloodshed. Much of the work that Vasconcelos was doing was based on information from the United States. But he did not do things halfway. He built good cases, and when he made an arrest, you could be sure that the subject would stay locked up. Today in Mexico, people are being arrested, but due to the lack of a functioning legal system, they are getting out in one or two years. The legal system can't keep them locked up. So what are they going to do then? They get out and go looking for the people they had problems with to settle the score. That results in even more bloodshed.

So, in terms of what happened with Dr. Oropeza, this signaled the beginning of the boom back in those years. The narcos wanted everyone to realize just what they were capable of. And now, with what happened to Vasconcelos, you realize that the narcos are still in control. "We do what we want. We go where we want." And if anyone challenges their power or tries to be equal to them, that person will realize that the narcos can handle it and they are capable of winning.

THE LIFE, 3

I depend directly on God . . . God is with me. While I was waiting outside just now, I read this:

> *Fear of man will prove to be a snare, but whoever trusts in the Lord is kept safe.* (Temer a los hombres resulta una trampa, pero el que confía en el Señor sale bien librado.)
> Proverbs 29:25

So I do not need to fear men, I need to trust in God. But I realize and I am eternally grateful for this confidence—that I am immensely privileged to be able to trust in God.

These men, Oropeza and Vasconcelos, in their time, each served their own god. For instance, Oropeza's god was doing his job as a journalist. And what did it get him? Death. For Vasconcelos, I think his god was to serve the government, to be subject to the government, and to carry out the orders he was given. And what did that get him? Death.

I serve the Lord, and I will follow Him on the same road.

But these men, despite the power of their words and their actions, they were brought down. Who is it that cannot be brought down?

It is a vision. No one is exempt. We are all just passing through this world. The only sure thing is that if we are born, we will also die. But there are very few lucky enough to die in their beds, asleep, without feeling a thing—to die happy. And to have lived a life that was good for their children, their grandchildren, and everyone else. God is good, and if we are lucky, we are allowed to have children and then grandchildren and we are able to enjoy them and be with them and we can say, "Thank you, God."

And be satisfied with our lives.

In the environment that I moved in, I never thought that I would live to see my children and grandchildren. Never never never. At any moment I could die in a hail of bullets. You carry out your job in fractions of a second, and you must be cold-blooded to do it. In the moment you must act without thinking. You must be full of malice and wickedness to do this work. And you must know what you are doing. But you never ever have time to think about having children and grandchildren.

You never have time to think about it. The future is always uncertain. Now, yes, thanks to God, I can make plans. In my past life, I never thought, "What shall we do for Christmas?" You have everything, but only in the moment. And you must enjoy it in the moment. Whatever you have, goes, goes, goes. You never expect to have a future.

Well, maybe only if you are a very high-ranking person. But even then, you have to know how to administer your resources and how to protect your loved ones.

I used to think . . . I remember once I told you: You never want to be either the head or the tail. Both get cut off. So you want to be the belly in order to be safe. But now I feel differently. Now I want to be the head, the point of the lance. Because we are the people of God. We are here because God is taking care of us. Our past is past. And people need to see us like we are now. I no longer want to be in the middle where things are easy and safe . . . that is the past. Now I want to be the head, the point of the lance. Oropeza and Vasconcelos also were both at the head, they were points of the lance. They were pioneers. One in journalism and the other in the police. And look at what happened to them.

• • •

There are others who have passed through these stages of the vicious circle and who want to do something. As I have drawn these charts for you, of ninety people, ninety elements who graduate from any class in an academy, fifty of them are involved with the narco-trafficking organizations. Whether they are in the ministerial police, the preventive police, the judicial police, the federal police, or elements of the army. I have reviewed for you how this works, how from the very beginning the narcos send remittances to these elements, investing in these people from the very beginning. The narcos realize that by paying these people early on, they are forming them, maintaining them, just like parents take care of their children. They will end up being much more faithful to the narcos than to the government or to the army because since they were children they have been maintained and taken care of by the narcos.

It is a family. We can say, like in any family, not everyone is involved. Maybe one person is, but not the whole family. But

from that one person, the disintegration of the entire family begins. The disintegration of the family begins with divorce and
causes many problems. The children are taken care of not by a
couple but by the mother or the father alone.

The government has no desire to resolve this problem, this
situation. The government does not try to stop the situation.
The government acts in the way that the narcos tell them to act.
The government conducts training, and the narcos defend themselves using the same government corporations.

This wall that the United States is building on the border
with Mexico? This wall is impressive, and built into this wall are
gates that will allow armored trucks to pass through. What does
this tell us? It tells us that in any moment, if the narco-trafficking
organizations actually take control in Mexico, the United States
will have its border well protected.

• • •

And speaking of people who are kidnapped, *los levantados*, even
if they have protection, they will always, always have to pay the
price. For every ten people who are kidnapped, if two of them
remain alive, it is because those two had a good relationship with
those in power, the narcos.

Remember that I showed you how a long time ago the narcos
already had cell phones that we called "bricks"? The narcos were
the only ones at the time who had the money to acquire this
equipment. Before any police had them, the narcos had them,
and they worked with American phone lines. No one else had
the resources to pay for them.

How is it possible to say, for example, when they have recovered some $200 million from a mansion in Mexico City, that the
narcos do not have a huge amount of money stored away? How

could $200 million be handled on the street? How could such huge amounts of money and drugs be moved around the country? How? That's an easy question. You do it with the help of the *authority*. And who has authority now? It belongs to the narco-trafficking organizations. It is a disgrace.

The government has already tried to take back some control from the cartels and has tried to begin in the prisons. And what has happened? There have been uprisings, not just in a few but in many prisons all over the country. Cynically, the narcos come and take people out of the prisons as if they were just going into their own houses, and they take out twenty or thirty people right under the noses of the government. It is all arranged.*

THE SYSTEM, 3

To be a sicario during that time became a real profession. But like I told you, it isn't like that any longer. Now you can look on the

---

* For example, the case came to light of a prison warden in the state of Durango who ran a group of killers from inside the prison who were released at night to carry out executions, including the spectacular massacre of seventeen people at a party outside the city of Torreón on July 18, 2010, more than a year after the sicario mentioned the role of the prisons in the work of the criminal organizations. Rory Carroll gave this account in *The Guardian* ("Mexico's Drugs War: In the City of Death," September 16, 2010): It was just another massacre in a country plagued by violence. But this time it was carried out by prison inmates—who'd been let out specially. "Who let them out?" barked the voice. "The director," replied the doomed man. The video ends minutes later with a shot to the head. A tortured confession would hardly be credible except that in this case it was true. The attorney general confirmed the story. Forensic results showed the massacre victims were shot with R-15 rifles—standard issue for prison guards. Federal authorities swooped on the prison and detained the guards. The director, a stout, formidable blonde named Margarita Rojas Rodriguez, who had recently been named "woman of the year 2010" by the state governor, was also arrested. "Disbelief. I just couldn't believe it. I had never heard of something like this," says Eduardo Olmos, Torreón's mayor.

Internet and find a sicario. You can find someone advertising: "You want to kill someone? I'm a sicario. I will do it for you for $5,000."

And you are supposed to believe that for $5,000 you can get somebody killed just because you don't like him? This started to happen a lot and then what? You would see cars all shot up like a pincushion. You would see people who are not even connected to narco-trafficking but who might be fighting over a stall in a flea market. In Mexico they might use bus drivers. But this is not the work of a sicario. This is the work of imitators.

The sicario knows his job. He knows exactly when to strike, he knows his objective. And the sicario would never, never advertise or publicize his work. He is someone who is always among the people. He has relationships with the people. He could be playing baseball with his kids or he could be attending a meeting in the town council at city hall. He knows how to behave, he knows how to dress. He knows how to conduct himself, he knows how to talk. He is well educated. This is what the narco-trafficking organizations know, and this is what they are willing to pay for by cultivating people in many places and for years, to ensure that their work is properly carried out.

When this stuff started happening on the Internet, not only did the source of money for killing people start to diminish, but also, you started to see something else. They created "a line," *La Linea*, and it has been operating now for years. And this "line" says: "All of you people, you are going to stop killing people." So what did "the line" do? They said, "So if you want to be imitators, you will be eliminated." And they began to eliminate a lot of people. And that began to create the problem that Mexico is living through right now, thanks to these imitators.

• • •

The narcos pay the investigative organizations. And the personnel of these organizations are the main eyes and ears of the narco-trafficking organizations. The government is in charge of training these people in the academies all over the Republic of Mexico, and they are then delivered to the narco-trafficking organizations, already trained and instructed in military tactics and ready for the battle. There are many different kinds of academies for specialized training, and many of those who are trained will go straight to work for the narcos. I will tell you that of fifty elements trained in the academies, at least fifteen are already mixed up with the narcos and another fifteen are just about to be corrupted. Because the police are so badly paid, what they would get in two weeks the narcos will pay in one day. It's that simple.

So what's happening? The narcos are empowered by this, and they have their eyes and ears everywhere. And the pressure on the Mexican government and the assistance received from the United States and other countries to do away with the narco-trafficking groups will never make any headway without the loyalty among the high government leaders.

• • •

The cartels no longer have the same control over the academies that they had in the past. Why? Because the people no longer want to join the police forces. The people no longer have any confidence, and they are afraid to join the police. They are afraid that if they join the police, they will face this choice: "Do you want us to pay you with gold? Or lead?" This is a nine-millimeter bullet.

He draws the bullet.

You either take the money, or we kill you.

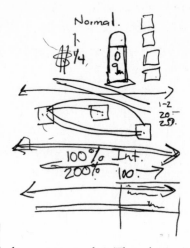

So what did they start to do? They began to bring people from other countries, such as *maras* [*marasalvatruchas*—gangsters from Central America]. They start to bring people from gangs in the United States. But there is one thing I can assure you: All of these people they are bringing in? They all have to be trained and instructed by sicarios who have learned it from the ground up. It is not very simple to let loose a group of one hundred or two hundred gangsters and expect that you can use them to control a city. That is very difficult, very difficult.

What you have to do, and what the narco-trafficking organizations are doing, is taking small groups of five or ten into the sierra to receive military training, and then letting them loose, here and there in the cities a few at a time. And then, little by little, they are killing and getting killed. How do they get to the cities? In planes and also in buses and trucks, overland.

So when you have these elements well trained and instructed, here he is:

He draws the sicario as he learns his craft.

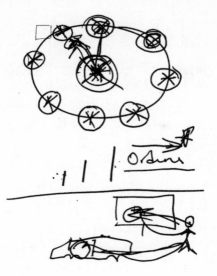

When he has passed through all of these little steps and tests—he goes through primary school, he learns to crawl, to walk, he begins to trot, to run, he can almost fly, now he has learned to fly—at this stage, when he is fully trained, you cannot ask him to do the same kind of work he did when he was barely crawling. That is really hard. Now he is trained to kill, to execute, and to do it well. He can no longer do the work of a beginner.

Remember that orders are carried out, not discussed. Unfortunately, sometimes there are errors in our plans. And the only one who can make a mistake is the boss. And since he is the boss, if he makes a mistake he can order the job to be done again. But if the sicario makes a mistake, no matter how big he is or how good he is at the job, he will also fall. That will be the end of him.

I mention that back in 1991—the year of Oropeza's murder— newspapers called it the bloodiest year in the city's history. A total of 134 people were murdered in 1991 in Juárez.

Wow! And now, in just one month, more than three hundred people are murdered.* Back in those days, it was rare to see an executed person on the street. Back then, there was some kind of respect. Now there is no respect. Respect is gone. But you have to consider that back then, in addition to counting the people who are murdered in the open, you also have to count the reports of disappeared persons. And there were many people disappeared that some years later come to light when clandestine burials are discovered. And many disappeared who were never counted.

I have seen foolish executions carried out by children. There is no longer any respect. Some kid will say, "I like this girl, but she is with you. . . . But I want her, she should be with me. . . ." And that can be enough for a murder . . . executions carried out by kids of fourteen, fifteen, sixteen years old. . . . Education must begin at home, but now the media, the TV news, the newspapers report all of this. Sure, it is better to have the information than to have it hidden like it was before, when only the privileged would have information. But this information must be handled very carefully.

What is the message that is being given out to the young kids now? In the media and on the Internet, the message sent out more than any other is "sicario, sicario, sicario, sicario, sicario, sicario" . . . so what happens is that every child wants to be a sicario. To be a sicario is a big deal. It comes out in the news that you can earn a lot of money, and it is easy for them since they are kids. So what do they have, really? Maybe in the moment, a little happiness and money. But they are completely destroying their lives. They don't realize it. But it is not a profession to be a sicario. At some time in the past, maybe there was some kind of

---

* A record was set in October 2010 when a total of 359 people were victims of homicide in Juárez.

professionalization, but now this idea of being a sicario is a game, a temptation, like when a child cries for something and you give him a popsicle just to make him happy in the moment.

It was very different back in the time of the operation against Dr. Oropeza. Plans were made. Very well-trained people were contracted, and every aspect of the job was checked out. Now there is such audacity. The level of corruption among the authorities is so high. Back then, there were many corrupt officials also, but not so many as now.

And what about Señor Vasconcelos? Maybe it was an accident after all, and the plane crashed. But what if it was an assassination? It was very well done if that is the case, if those pilots were part of the plot. Because these people who were killed were very important to the president—these men were very close to him. Mouriño was a man he trusted, they say one of his closest friends, like a member of his family. I think that the president of Mexico must be very careful of who he places in these high positions. It is as if they are his family and he must depend on them for his peace and his security. No one, not even a minor narco boss, will allow his family to be touched. But this president is careless, and he has allowed these things to happen to those closest to him, like his secretary of Interior [*Gobernación*], and so he seems weak and things will keep on happening to him. This man was like a member of the president's family and so Calderón realizes that he has been hit and that they will continue to attack him. He makes agreements. Or he allows others to make agreements with some narcos and not with others.

This government is very vulnerable. The narcos will continue to be on the attack. The government has some successes, but only up to a point. The successes have mostly been due to the experiments that the DEA is carrying out now in Mexico, and the president is doing what the DEA orders. I think that the United States law enforcement needs to take advantage of the Calderón government, because he will allow them to do whatever investigation they want. Many other governments will not allow them to go so far. Another government will not allow the same cooperation and the availability of their military to work with the United States. The United States needs to take advantage of this situation.

Sadly, some good men become casualties in this system. Many years ago, Oropeza was a man who published his articles in a newspaper here on the border, and many people read them. His articles were strong, clear, and concise. His punches really hit home. No one ever knew where he got the information that he published, but it was always strong and clear. And for being a strong, clear, and concise journalist, he was killed. In the same way, Señor Vasconcelos, for being a good policeman—clear, honest, and concise—he was killed also.

THE LIFE, 4

So what are you left with? What can you do? You try to keep yourself in the middle, you try to maintain a balance. And you know what? Sometimes this balance is right there for us, and it passes us by and we don't even know it.

That is what happened to me. I saw these signs, these big, luminous messages. I would see them along the way to the places I was sleeping, the places I was staying. I did not understand what these signs meant at this time in my life. It was when I had stopped drinking, smoking, and using drugs.

At this time, I was sleeping in different places. I was not sleeping at home because I did not trust myself. I was afraid I might do something to harm my family. What were these signs, these announcements? It was something I had seen in all of my dreams, and it was like a mixed-up reprise, a *revoltura*, of all the things I had done in my life.

And so I started to gather together money that I had put away here and there in various bank accounts, hidden in different places so that I would be okay. And I sent money to my house so that my family would be okay. But it isn't good enough just to send money home. Money doesn't raise children. The father figure in the home is what is needed to raise your children. Money does not raise children.

> *He bangs on the tablet as he says this. And he begins*
> *a kind of dialogue with himself. . . .*

In these moments you don't realize—when you are trying to clean up your act—when you keep seeing these signs. . . .

"So, hey, what is going on with you?"

"They are following me."

"You are a professional. You know that they are going to kill you, but it is not the right moment because you haven't done anything yet. And you have not made any mistakes."

What you did was to quit your bad habits—you quit drinking, smoking, and taking drugs, and sometimes fooling around with women. When you leave these things behind, it's strange, because it changes your attitude. But what is really strange is that everywhere you look you start to see all these little signs. And I'm not going to tell you that these are signs that say, "You have to come to this church," or, "You have to join this religion. . . ."

No, these are little signs that say:

CALL IF YOU NEED HELP. *HE* IS WAITING FOR YOU.

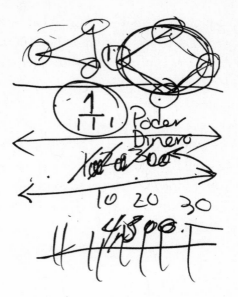

And you run into these signs everywhere. And you can see them everywhere. You can even see them from your house.

When fear arrives at your own home, when you fear for your own family, when you have to sleep in other houses so that you will not hurt your own family. . . . This fear becomes not cowardice, *cobardia*, rather, it becomes courage and fortitude, passion and rage, *coraje*.* First, it is triangulated courage, three-sided courage. And then a circle that encloses you.

And then you realize that, yes, there is hope and, yes, there is salvation. And that this salvation cannot be controlled by a man. A man whose only accomplishment, whose only achievement, is to have power and money. And he has so much, he possesses such abundance, that he always wants more. And more. And more.

---

* *Coraje* means all of these things in Spanish—courage and fortitude as well as passion and rage. It is usually spoken to mean one or the other, not both. But in this case, I believe the sicario intended all of these meanings.

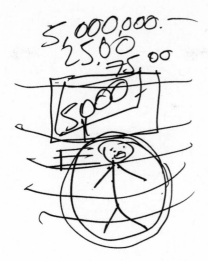

And it does not matter to him that in acquiring such power and money that one or two or three die. . . . But it is never only one or two or three. No, it is 100 or 200 or 300 people. . . . It doesn't even matter to him if it is 4,500 people whose lives are on his conscience. All that matters to him is that he can say: "I am in control, I am the one who gives the orders, *yo soy el que manda*."

• • •

But every day there are these little signs that distract you and guide you day after day. And you realize now that the only thing your bosses are offering you is $500 or $1,000 so that you will keep watch over some stupid little car all day. Or that you are just "the Eyes" watching to see if someone passes by, and you have to wait around all day for nothing. When you know that, instead of being the Eyes, you could be earning $5,000 to execute somebody. You could be getting paid $25,000, $75,000. There are people with prices on their heads worth up to $5 million. People who are on the run and people they are looking for.

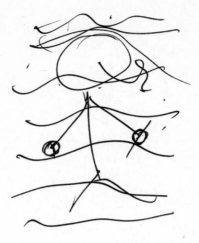

And now you realize that to everyone—to the organization, to the bosses—what you really are is *nothing*.

You realize that you are completely alone in the world. All you have is a weapon in each hand. But if you end up out in the cold with nothing, you are not going to find anyone, there will be no one who will be close to you or who will protect you. You are alone. There is no one. Except, if you have one, your family may be there with you.

And the only One who will be looking after your family is The Lord, *El Señor*. It will not be anyone who calls himself "Master," or someone who dares to call himself "Boss," "Patron," "Number One," or "Bad Ass" [*Fregon*].

None of these can compare with the One who through all of the filth that you have been living all of this time has been guarding and taking care of your family. And He is waiting to tell you that there is hope. And there is hope to get you out of this. And that if you accept Him, He will accept you. And that nothing, none of this, will ever affect you in your life anymore.

You must take precautions. You must be very careful. You must be jealous. Not jealous of your wife, but jealous of your actions. Because this Lord who is the Ruler of everything, is jealous of His children, and He loves them, and He protects all of His children.

When you encounter Him and He gives you peace and He reunites you with the half of what you have lost—your family and the person you really are—and they are united in the Holy Trinity and they are with the Lord, you know what? This peace and tranquility that you live in this moment begins to grow, and you become a new man. And this new man is not afraid of any other man. He fears only God.

And to the man who calls himself "Patron,"
To the man who calls himself "The Boss,"
To the man who calls himself "Number One,"
To the man who calls himself "Master" . . .
What are they masters of?
Masters of shit!

↑ Hombre Nuevo.
Temor. — Hombre
Dios.
Patron, Jefe, Maestro ✗

When God called me, He made me roll around in all of this filth. He took away the very last cent that I had made from all of this.

He flips back again through the notebook of his life.

He took away my clothes.
He took away my thoughts.
He took away everything.
He shook me down.
And you know what?
He left me with nothing but my own skin, naked, together
    with my family.
And from there, we can begin a new life in Him.

POSTSCRIPT
AUTOEXILIO (SELF-EXILE)

THE SICARIO

April 2010

For a long time I have watched with sadness that the reality of Mexico and Mexicans is to endure all of the errors committed on a continuing basis by the political leaders of this country. I wonder what would have become of me and my family if in some moment of desperation I had decided not to abandon Mexico and the small amount of money and property that I had there. Let me tell you:

203

A certain commander told me back in those years, "Trust us. We are the only ones who can defend you with your declaration. We will clarify some cases, and you are a witness, and if you do not do it, we will be able to arrest you and accuse you of complicity."

Disgracefully, *desgraciadamente*, I trusted him, and less than four hours later the woman who at that time was my partner was injured, she was raped and gasoline was poured on her, and though she survived, she was left in this condition as a very clear message to me. At that time, I decided to hide in a distant state in Mexico and cut all connections to friends and family and to forget them. At that time, I then began to work honestly, day after day, until I was able to save a small amount of money that gave me the solvency I needed to be able to move on, to get ahead.

I did not have much, but the little that I had was enough to live well. I met a beautiful person, and after some time passed, we decided to get married, and in order to do this legally, I had to give precise information about my date of birth and address to the justice of the peace [civil registry] where we got married. They found me in less than three days, and sadly, disgracefully, this is when I realized the extent to which the Mexican government was infiltrated by the dirty business of trade in weapons and drugs. That is when I realized that they had a video of my face, that they could find me and identify me even when I had only given general information to the civil registry so that I could get married. But that was enough for them to find me. Could it be that the criminals have better operational systems than the government? Or that the operational systems of the country are at the disposal of the narcos who are working for them?

I made the decision then to approach a certain person and tell him what was happening to me. To do this, I had to move again with all of my family. Now it was not just my life that was in danger, but also the life of the woman I had just married.

I told this person that I had decided to ask for help, and he gave me some good advice. I tried at that moment to seek protection from the federal government, but unfortunately, things were even worse than in the first instance. The federal authorities had given themselves the job of ransacking houses and detaining people linked to narco-trafficking and smuggling. These people were being bought off, and not satisfied with that, they gave the criminals my description and told them that it was me who had given the authorities the necessary information for their arrest and detention. I should mention that I had not turned over any information on any of these people. But they were detained, and the merchandise that they were trafficking in was confiscated, their money was taken, and later they were set free, and of course they then began an infernal hunt for me and my family.

This caused panic, not only in my immediate family but also among other relatives, because by this time they were already keeping us under surveillance—the homes of some of our close relatives were being watched.

Again, I decided that I would confide in someone, and that person was Señor Vasconcelos, but I never had the opportunity to meet with him. He was assassinated along with the secretary of *Gobernación* [*Interior*]. Perhaps, if I had had this chance, it would have changed my life. I do not know. But what I do know is that since that moment I have been fleeing from Mexico, and I have no desire to return for any reason.

Disgracefully, everything in that country is evil. There is so much corruption that it can have no end, no matter how much help Mexico gets from other countries. This stuff about the president of the Republic is pure farce. Looking on from my vantage point, I am so disillusioned. He is just a puppet manipulated by his ministers. Unfortunately, there is no need for him to commit himself to any Mexican, since he is already completely committed only to his own interests, just like many former presidents, and he is just the tip of the iceberg.

A very good friend of mine who has also left the country and is living in self-imposed exile from Mexico looked back in sadness at the fact that he had worked for a certain government official of Juárez.

My friend told me the following, and I have his authorization to record it here. This is his story:

That day I was in the foyer of the official's office waiting to see him, when about eight men arrived. It looked like they were armed, and only one of them was carrying a briefcase. They asked to speak with the official, but his personal secretary did not let them in to see him. So then one of them made a phone call, and just after that, the official came out of his office to receive him personally, and he reprimanded his secretary for having obstructed this person's access to his office. This person handed over the briefcase to the official. And after that I saw the man in his office, standing right next to his chair. But what happened to the secretary? He was scolded and punished so much that he decided to quit his job. At this moment, to the surprise of everyone there and to the surprise of the official's personal secretary, we found out that the person who the secretary had tried to deny access to speak to the government official was the narco-trafficker in charge of the plaza of Ciudad Juárez and of the state of Chihuahua.

Imagine how many of these corrupt politicians there are out there! Now they are cloning themselves. . . . I hope that the citizens of that city that has been so beaten, defeated, terrorized by narco-trafficking will not commit the same error again!

My friend, like myself, we now see all of this with great sadness, and we can never again speak with any of the Mexican authorities. Now they are all mixed up in narco-trafficking, those that are not are murdered, like Señor Vasconcelos and the secretary of *Gobernación* [Mouriño] were murdered. I think that he was an intimate friend of President Felipe Calderón. The secretary paid very dearly for this friendship.

The sicario made the following comment in response to recent elections in the state of Chihuahua and the subsequent murder of a Juárez official:

God bless you. . . .

Disgracefully, the people of Juárez decided to vote again for a kangaroo, to not call him what he really is, a rat who walks on two legs—a person who is not far removed from the intrigue and dirty dealings of the underworld of the city. And in part he is the protector along with another group of people who shelter under his wing. They think they are beyond reach of the law, they think they are vaccinated and immune, but the truth is, it isn't like that. . . . Soon we'll all be living in the crazy house. . . . Two or three losses have struck his team already before he takes power, but this is nothing except to remind him who is paying him and that he had better obey. This seems to be what's happening, and again with this election, there will follow another three years of robbery with complete impunity. . . . The criminals will be reorganizing themselves inside the police, all in secret, just like before he manipulated the police in Juárez. . . . And in addition to all this, what has been happening will not end because every day there are more and more payments arriving from people who are defending the little they have left, which was once their patrimony but has been stripped from them in their towns and villages.

BENEDICTION

The documentary film El Sicario, Room 164, *directed by Gianfranco Rosi, was shown on French and German television in late November 2010. The film has won numerous awards since its premiere in Venice. The sicario expressed his feelings with these words:*

May God bless you.

How grateful I am for this news about the documentary. It seems to me that it is having a good premiere and exposure in the media, and above all it shows us a part of the realism that many of us wish to forget, because of the violence that Mexico is living through. Thanks for giving to all a little bit of realism, and we keep hoping that the government of Mexico will one day really put things right and not continue to join forces with these people.

Saludos and be well this Thanksgiving.

May Jesus Christ fill you with blessings.

Mama, put my guns in the ground
I can't shoot them anymore. . . .

—Bob Dylan, "Knockin' on Heaven's Door"